*Beginning Secondary School*
*Teacher's Guide*

# BEGINNING SECONDARY SCHOOL TEACHER'S GUIDE

## Some Problems and Suggested Solutions

## Melvin Keene

UNIVERSITY
PRESS OF
AMERICA

LANHAM • NEW YORK • LONDON

Copyright © 1969 by

Melvin Keene

University Press of America,® Inc.

4720 Boston Way
Lanham, MD 20706

3 Henrietta Street
London WC2E 8LU England

This edition reprinted in 1985 by University Press of America, Inc. by arrangement with Harper & Row, Publishers, Inc.

Library of Congress Cataloging in Publication Data

Keene, Melvin.
    Beginning secondary school teacher's guide.

    Reprint. Originally published: New York : Harper &
Row, c1969.
    Bibliography: p.
    Includes index.
    1. High school teaching. 2. High school teachers.
3. First year teachers. I. Title.
LB1607.K36   1985        373.11'02        85-9074
ISBN 0-8191-4668-4 (pbk. : alk. paper)

*This book is dedicated to the thousands of boys and girls who have been in my classes. They are deep in my heart. It is my prayer that a full measure of what they taught me will help you.*

# Contents

*Section Two:*
YOUR STUDENT

*7. Handling Troublemakers*    *121*

*Section Three:*
## YOUR ATTITUDE

*Section Five:*
## YOUR FELLOW TEACHERS

### 14. Pointers for Professional Well-being 197

### 15. Meeting Personality Problems with Other Teachers 204

# Preface

## 1. *The audience for this book*

This guide is especially designed to give *practical* help to the college student training to be a teacher in either a junior or senior high school. Because secondary school supervisors are usually so hard pressed by the many facets of administration, they rarely are able to devote as much time as they'd like to assist young teachers over their first hurdles. All too frequently an inexperienced teacher endures distressful situations that could have been avoided. Moreover, some of the *practical* suggestions in this book may open a different approach and new horizons to some experienced secondary school teachers. Professionally, most of us can always learn something new.

## 2. *What this book offers you*

This book carefully identifies many specific problems and offers hundreds of definite suggestions based on twenty-nine years' experience in secondary schools. Situations which need skillful handling are dealt with in a down-to-earth manner suggesting possible ways to deal with problems under actual classroom conditions, especially in difficult schools. The chapters are grouped into sections for easy reference on a particular problem. Thus, a check with the table of contents will give you immediate assistance. I trust that a degree of professional inspiration is present, but my emphasis is definitely on the *practical*. The intent is for you to utilize this guide every day as problems confront you. By its steady use, your ability to control pupil and school situations will be developed.

In the first reading from the opening chapter to the end of the guide, you will become aware of repetition. However, this is a deliberate, consistent plan and a significant contribution of the book. Ordinarily repetition is boring, but in this handbook it is used to strengthen the various aspects and interweaving of the many complex factors that a beginning teacher usually faces. A given classroom situation or a particular problem with a student often employs factors from other situations and problems. This complexity frequently eliminates the possibility of isolating controlling factors. They are commonly present in many important patterns of behavior presented to the beginning teacher. Therefore, major points are deliberately repeated to impress the beginner with their importance as they reappear in different situations.

## 3. *Limitations*

Of course not all situations can be reduced to a solution by a simple set of suggestions. Nor can all problems be solved for all new teachers in all schools. But this guide will possibly help you through many of the important problems you may face in your probationary period.

No two schools are exactly alike. In fact, the suburban and city schools frequently vary considerably. There is a tremendous range in administrative organization, supervision, student and faculty abilities, socioeconomic backgrounds, teaching philosophies, and so forth. From this wide range of personalities and conditions, complex situations develop. Consequently it is foolish to expect that any handbook could hope to provide precise remedies for all difficulties that could conceivably face every secondary school teacher in the United States. Furthermore, I freely admit that every situation may have its own aspects. Indeed, sometimes we find contrasting advice from competent, experienced teachers on a given problem. This book does not claim to provide an answer to *all* of your problems. But as a beginner you have little or no experience to help you, except for perhaps a short term of student-teaching. Therefore, the 551 *definite* suggestions in this book may prove a valuable guide. The 146 *practical* topics may provide you with an understanding of some of the fundamental problems you may meet. To underscore its *practical* goal, this book is written in a concise, colloquial style that uses informal writing to come to the point in as few words as possible. Lengthy anecdotes have been avoided. No attempt is made to cover in depth the broad fields of educational philosophy, psychology, measurements, guidance, subject techniques, general methods, or specialized areas. Each of these branches is a complete subject in itself that requires its own study. A list of suggested, up-to-date books in these areas has been added as a supplement for your convenience. Briefly, this book is limited to giving you down-to-earth advice.

## 4. *Terminology*

You can easily adjust the terminology to your particular school. Thus, a guidance counselor may be referred to as a grade adviser, the supervisor of discipline as the dean, the subject supervisor as the chairman or head of department.

MELVIN KEENE

# *Acknowledgments*

I wish to express my appreciation to the following New York City educators for their critical reading of the manuscript: Mr. Joseph Bellafiore, principal of New Dorp High School; Mr. James F. Corbett, principal of Curtis High School; Mr. Raymond Halloran, principal of Tottenville High School; Mrs. Josephine Landes, chairman of nursing sciences for Richmond high schools; Professor Louis P. Raichle, of Staten Island Community College; and to my wife, Alice, teacher of English at Edwin Markham Junior High School.

In addition my special thanks go to Dr. Marvin D. Alcorn, Professor of Education at San Diego State College; to Dr. Jean D. Grambs, Professor of Education, University of Maryland; to Dr. Paul M. Halverson, Professor of Education, The University of Georgia; to Dr. Harold C. Hand, Professor of Education (retired), University of Illinois; to Dr. Kenneth H. Hoover, Professor of Education, Arizona State University; and to Dr. Raymond E. Schultz, Professor of Higher Education, Florida State University, for their many detailed, excellent suggestions and for their careful analytical evaluations of the manuscript.

Furthermore I wish to express my sincere appreciation to Dr. Thomas J. Brown, Chairman, Department of Secondary Education, Hofstra University; to Dr. James J. Gallagher, Associate Director, Institute for Research on Exceptional Children, University of Illinois; to Dr. John W. Loughary, Associate Professor, School of Education, University of Oregon; to Dr. Ralph

L. Mosher, Assistant Professor, Graduate School of Education, Harvard University; to Dr. William W. Wattenberg, Department of Educational Psychology, Wayne State University; and to Dr. Paul Woodring, Department of Psychology, Western Washington State College, for their analytical reading of the outline of the book and the first chapter, and their many helpful comments.

The assistance of all of these reviewers is gratefully acknowledged. Any inadequacy, error, or conflicting viewpoint is entirely my own responsibility.

Also I wish to thank the many professors of education in colleges and universities throughout the United States who encouraged me to write a practical handbook for beginning teachers in secondary schools and offered suggestions. In particular:

Dr. William M. Alexander, Chairman, Curriculum and Instruction, University of Florida

Dr. Dwight W. Allen, Associate Professor of Education, Stanford University

Dr. Lester W. Anderson, Professor of Education, University of Michigan

Dr. David P. Ausubel, Professor of Educational Psychology, University of Illinois

Dr. Warren R. Baller, Professor of Educational Psychology, University of Nebraska

Dr. John A. Bartky, Dean, School of Education, Stanford University

Dr. Charles S. Benson, Professor of Education, University of California at Berkeley

Dr. Ruyard K. Bent, Professor of Education, University of Arkansas

Dr. George Z. F. Bereday, Professor of Comparative Education, Columbia University

Dr. Bruce J. Biddle, Associate Professor of Psychology and Sociology, University of Missouri

Dr. Benjamin S. Bloom, Professor of Education, University of Chicago

Dr. Merl E. Bonney, Professor of Psychology, North Texas State University

Dr. Nelson L. Bossing, Distinguished Visiting Professor, Southern Illinois University

Dr. Angelo V. Boy, Associate Professor of Education, University of New Hampshire

Dr. Theodore Brameld, Professor of Educational Philosophy, Boston University

Dr. Robert N. Bush, Professor of Education, Co-Director of Research, Stanford University

Dr. William E. Cole, Professor of Sociology, University of Tennessee

Dr. Arthur W. Combs, Professor of Education, University of Florida

Dr. David R. Cook, Associate Professor of Counselor Education, Northeastern University

Dr. Lee J. Cronbach, Professor of Education and Psychology, Stanford University

Dr. John P. DeCecco, Associate Professor of Psychology, San Francisco State College

Dr. Stan Dropkin, Associate Professor of Education, Queens College, City University of New York

Dr. R. Oliver Gibson, Professor of Education, State University of New York at Buffalo

Dr. Edward C. Glanz, Provost, Southampton College, Long Island University

Dr. Marvin D. Glock, Professor of Education, Cornell University

Dr. John A. Green, Assistant Dean, College of Education, University of Idaho

Dr. Earl W. Harmer, Professor of Education, University of Utah

Dr. Robert J. Havighurst, Professor of Urban Education, Fordham University

Dr. Glenn R. Hawkes, Associate Dean, University of California at Davis

Dr. Henry J. Hermanowicz, Dean, College of Education, Illinois State University

Dr. Tyrus Hillway, Professor of Higher Education, Colorado State College

Dr. Philip L. Hosford, Professor of Teacher Education, New Mexico State University

Dr. Herold C. Hunt, Eliot Professor of Education, Graduate School, Harvard University

Dr. William J. Iverson, Professor of Education, Stanford University

Dr. G. Orville Johnson, Professor of Social Education, Syracuse University

Dr. C. Gratton Kemp, Professor of Education, Ohio State University

Dr. Samuel A. Kirk, Professor of Special Education, University of Arizona

Dr. Herbert J. Klausmeier, Co-Director, Research and Development Center for Learning and Re-Education, University of Wisconsin

Dr. George F. Kneller, Professor of Education, University of California at Los Angeles

Dr. Gordon C. Lee, Dean, College of Education, University of Washington

Dr. Dan C. Lortie, Associate Professor of Education, University of Chicago

Dr. L. Morris McClure, Associate Dean, College of Education, University of Maryland

Dr. Fred McKinney, Professor of Psychology, University of Missouri

Dr. Carroll H. Miller, Professor of Education, Northern Illinois University

Dr. Harold E. Mitzel, Assistant Dean for Research, College of Education, Pennsylvania State University

Dr. Clyde B. Moore, Professor of Education, Cornell University

Dr. Harry R. Moore, Professor, Colorado Seminary, University of Denver

Dr. Van Cleve Morris, Professor of Education, University of Illinois at Chicago

Dr. George J. Mouly, Professor of Education, University of Miami

Dr. Merle M. Ohlsen, Professor of Educational Psychology, University of Illinois

Dr. Wayne Otto, Associate Professor of Education, University of Wisconsin

Dr. David E. Purpel, Director, Programs in Teaching, Harvard University

Dr. Herman G. Richey, Secretary, National Society for the Study of Education, University of Chicago

Dr. Harry N. Rivlin, Dean of Teacher Education, City University of New York

Dr. Roy W. Roberts, Professor of Vocational Teacher Education, University of Arkansas

Dr. Benjamin M. Sachs, Professor of Educational Administration, Sacramento State College

Dr. Charles F. Schuller, Director, Instructional Media Center, Michigan State University

Dr. C. Leland Smith, Professor of Education, University of Kentucky

Dr. Frederick R. Smith, Professor of Education, Indiana University

Dr. Arthur W. Staats, Professor of Educational Psychology, University of Wisconsin

Dr. John Starkey, Associate Professor of Secondary Education, Northern Illinois University

Dr. John M. Stephens, Professor of Education, Johns Hopkins University

Dr. Lawrence H. Stewart, Professor of Education, University of California at Berkeley

Dr. Lindley J. Stiles, Dean, School of Education, University of Wisconsin

Dr. Michael J. Stolee, Associate Professor of Education, University of Miami

Dr. Florence B. Stratemeyer, Professor of Education, Eastern Kentucky University

Dr. Lawrence G. Thomas, Professor of Education, Stanford University

Dr. Walter A. Thurber, Division of Science Teaching, Syracuse University

Dr. Robert S. Thurman, Professor of Education, University of Tennessee

Dr. William Clark Trow, Professor of Education, University of Michigan

Dr. William Van Til, Coffman Distinguished Professor in Education, Indiana State University

Dr. Charles F. Warnath, Director, Counseling Center, Oregon State University

Dr. Sam P. Wiggins, Dean, College of Education, Cleveland State University

Dr. Richard L. Willey, Dean, College of Education, Idaho State University

Dr. John Withall, Head, Department of Secondary Education, Pennsylvania State University

Dr. Israel Woronoff, Professor of Education, Eastern Michigan University

Dr. C. Gilbert Wrenn, Professor of Education, Arizona State University

*Beginning Secondary School
Teacher's Guide*

# IMPORTANT COMMENTS
# FOR A BETTER UNDERSTANDING
# OF THIS GUIDE

1. Classroom control is strongly emphasized because frequently it may be one of the weak spots in a beginning teacher's ability to handle students, especially if the youngsters are already prone to misconduct. It is true that sometimes a new teacher may find himself in a select superior school where classroom control is a minor factor. But in the average school there is often a possibility that he may come in contact with some classes that are sometimes not easy for a beginner to manage. In addition there sometimes is the chance that he may receive his first position in a difficult school in a tough urban district. Furthermore, it sometimes may happen that a beginning teacher may have received his student-teacher practice for only a few weeks and even that possibly in a carefully chosen, well-controlled class under the expert guidance of an experienced teacher, so that he has little or no preparation with which to face serious control problems that he may encounter when he is on his own. Indeed, sometimes the beginner may receive little or no constructive help in control problems and may find himself very largely in a swim-or-perish situation. Anyone who has had practical experience in teaching difficult classes in a school where control is a major problem will usually admit that a beginning teacher should come well prepared to cope with such a situation. Of course it is conceded that the real key to control and maximizing learning is good teaching—the teaching of meaningful content in a

way that makes it possible for students to learn something important to them. But before the new teacher can achieve that goal, he usually needs the cooperation of his students. In some situations in some of our difficult city schools the cooperation of teen-agers may be difficult to obtain without an initial firm classroom control. Another possibility is that the beginner may start his career in a select superior school with top-quality classes and later on find himself in a different school—perhaps because of the inducement of a considerable salary increase—where classes are not so easy to control. Or, even in a given average secondary school, especially in large cities, there is possibly a considerable variation in the type of classes a new teacher may get from one term or year to the next. All in all, it seems generally advisable for a beginning teacher to have helpful suggestions for obtaining firm class control *should he need it*. As a rule a beginning teacher should realize the possibility of control problems that he may someday be forced to deal with. College professors giving education courses in methods have generally been aware that in their classes there may be some students who will be appointed to difficult schools where specific suggestions will be welcomed by a beginning teacher. Customarily the techniques of actual practice are needed as well as fundamental principles. It is admitted that procedures which contrast to those suggested may be equally successful. The problem of class control, as a case in point, has many approaches. But the suggestions made may be helpful to the beginning teacher having difficulty controlling his classes. What is said of value to teachers who are entering some of the very large schools in the difficult areas of big cities may have little or no application in many select suburban schools where a very different relationship with students is set up.

　　2. Repetition of suggestions will be found throughout the book. The beginning teacher should be able to refer to any section and get helpful advice on a particular problem. Another advantage of repetition is that important points are emphasized. Thus, repetition is an essential structure of this handbook. From the first page to the last, there is an almost constant interweaving of many factors in various possible combinations that enter into a number of situations. Because this guide is a reference

book, repetition should prove no problem after the first reading —when it may be somewhat tiresome. But the repetition is needed if the beginner is to be given a comprehensive understanding of the topic that concerns him *at the moment*. We are not so concerned with making this guide pleasant, easy reading —although we hope it has some of that quality—as that it prove itself truly helpful to the beginning teacher *under actual working conditions*.

3. List after list of possible suggestions—some of considerable length—may make for boredom. However, this handbook is not intended as a smooth-flowing text but as a supplement where the essential factors and suggestions are pointed out as concisely as possible to get to the point yet preserve clarity. The beginning teacher may frequently find a list of possible suggestions on a given situation a helpful guide and an easy reference.

4. It is generally acknowledged that a beginning teacher's psychological attitudes and his school environment tend to determine what he or she can or cannot do. Consequently there can be no guarantee that what works for one successful teacher will be applicable for someone else. Still, there may be a good deal of hard-headed wisdom in the other fellow's viewpoint and his recommendations as to what would be helpful. Thus the suggestions made in this handbook are but one set of answers illustrative of the range of problems and possible solutions. It is understood that individual effectiveness is quite different from generalizable validity. A beginning teacher should not conclude that if he does this and that, following suggestions so and so, he will automatically solve his problem. *One needs detailed knowledge of the particular situation:* type of learners, teacher's ability, curriculum, and their unique interaction. In spite of this weakness, there may be considerable help in the form of a handbook type of presentation where definite suggestions are made. Very often to the beginner a few suggestions may be of considerable assistance even though the approach pointed out is not necessarily the only solution to the problem.

5. Anecdotes from practical experience to be analyzed in terms of what might be done are eliminated. The aim of this

handbook is not to suggest ramifications of certain actions and to let the beginning teacher decide for himself upon a course of action. The purpose of this guide is *to give him positive suggestions to help him solve some of his problems*.

6. The apprehensive beginner is likely to feel overwhelmed by the problems with which this handbook confronts him, but any book dealing with problems is likely to seem depressing and discouraging. The fact is, however, that by mastering the negative aspects we can assert a positive attitude. Most beginners will find it a comfort to receive helpful suggestions when they have a problem.

7. Some suggestions made can be expected to be challenged by experienced teachers. But teachers are by no means in total agreement with themselves. Procedures that some applaud are frowned upon by others. This is true even within a single school.

8. Sometimes suggestions are made in the form of what not to do. This may be equally helpful with what to do. At times such suggestions may give a negative approach, but there are occasions when this is sometimes advisable.

9. This handbook should not implant a fear of adolescents. To the contrary, it should develop a liking for youngsters through understanding their problems and how to help them in the many situations frequently found in a complex modern secondary school. The beginning teacher needs to deal reasonably with teen-agers and this tone should be held in mind throughout the entire use of the handbook.

10. A colloquial style of writing is used with loose sentence structure for brevity and sparkle with a sprinkling of appropriate slang. This manner of presentation is not to speak down to the beginning teacher, nor to oversimplify—assuredly not to insult the intelligence of the reader—but to try to deal with the problems in a natural way and possibly make for easier reading of reference material that ordinarily may tend to become pedantic.

11. A new teacher frequently needs reassurance, support, and helpful guidance and the detailed observations, suggestions, and admonitions may well serve this purpose. This handbook

strives for a warm, friendly relationship with youngsters but a firm hand if the situation warrants it. The book may be inspiring at times—an important asset for helping a new teacher—but always very practical. The reader possibly may get the feeling that he has listened to a kind Dutch uncle.

## Section One
# YOUR CLASS

*In this section important factors are considered for getting your classes started properly so that control is established and the foundation for good instruction is put down.*

# CHAPTER 1

# *Developing a Good Learning Atmosphere*

*1. Need for organization on opening day. Fourteen important steps for efficient procedure. Why the first day is important.*

One of the secrets of success in teaching is frequently organization. It is generally advisable to plan what you are going to do and how you are going to do it. Seldom is planning of more importance than on the opening day, when you first meet your students. It may be that you, like many other beginners, understandably have a sense of insecurity. Therefore, it should help you to have everything planned carefully. It may be helpful to write down the following schedule and make it a part of your plan for use on your first day.

1. As soon as the class has assembled and the bell for the beginning of the period has sounded, introduce yourself (pronounce your name slowly and distinctly) and write your name on the board. If your name is odd or difficult to pronounce, say it again to make it easier for them.

2. Have slips of paper (3 by 6), or printed class cards available at some schools, ready. Distribute the slips or cards.

3. On the chalkboard print the following.

*Family name*                    *First Name*
*Homeroom* (in some schools called register or section room)
*Father's first name* (mother's or guardian's name if father is deceased)
*Address*
*Phone number* (if none, say so)
*Guidance counselor* (sometimes freshmen don't know who he is and
    you will have to obtain this information later; in some schools the
    counselor is called the grade adviser)
*Class* (the period the student reports to you)
*Date*
*Special notes:* (hobbies, clubs, teams, and other activities)

Make it clear that the more you know about each student, the
more you can help him. Take this opportunity to make an early
demonstration that you care about each of your students.

    4. Ask the students to give you the information above,
using ink and printing neatly, on the slips. Show them which way
you want the slips held so they will be uniform and easier for you
to use. Have some extra pens to lend to any students who may
come unprepared.

    5. Collect slips in order, separating each row with a
paper clip, so that you know immediately who is sitting where. A
word of advice: Take the trouble to collect the slips yourself, in-
specting them as you do, to be sure they are made out properly.

    6. If students have program cards that must be signed
by you, you can do that at the same time you collect the slips.

    7. Check the count of slips against the number of stu-
dents present. (It is not advisable to pass a sheet of paper around
the class, or even down each row, and ask the students to sign
their names. If you do, in some schools where the conduct of
teen-agers is sometimes a problem, you may find the signature of
"Snow White," or some youngster may not sign at all!) Of course
at the end of the day, you should rule off a seating chart, giving
the name and location of each student in that class. A seating
plan book with cards could also be used. Whichever method you
use, generally the most important single piece of business on the
first day is to *know the name of every student and exactly where
he sits.*

8. Have two or three students distribute textbooks and book-receipt cards. Collect receipts and check against the register so you are sure none are missing. If you are working on a curtailed schedule the first day, it probably would be advisable to omit book distribution and go directly to the next step. Of course it may be that students purchase their books in your state.

9. Have an assignment sheet ready with at least one week's work on it. Be specific. Give the number, date, and day the assignment is due. The first assignment is extremely important. It should be fun, interesting, involving, and something everyone can learn something from. Furthermore, the first assignment should be short and not dependent on a textbook. Distribute the assignment sheets. Motivate the students to want to do the first assignment—work out why it is important to them. Give the assignment in a friendly manner, taking the trouble to explain it carefully. Thus the students will generally get the impression that you are cordial but you mean business. This procedure tends to set the tone for your relationship with them for the entire term or year, as the case may be in your school organization.

10. Make changes in seating arrangement that seem obviously necessary. Be sure to shift the slips you collected into the proper row for any change you make. For example, a small, thin girl may be seated behind a tall, broad-shouldered boy. Or a student wearing thick eyeglasses may be in the far corner of the room and should be moved forward. It is advisable to suggest that students with special problems, such as a hearing defect, see you after class for seat preference. Of course further adjustments can be made the following day if necessary. Attendance from now on should simply be a matter of glancing at an empty seat, checking against seating plan, and recording absence. Many inexperienced teachers seem to feel that somehow they impress a class by pompously calling the roll each day—a waste of time. For informal situations, such as a gym or athletic field, attendance may be quickly taken by squads or in formation by numbers.

11. Give them something *definite* and *interesting* on their first day in your class. For example, start a class discussion on the topic assigned for that night's homework. The point is, the

students should leave your class the *first* day realizing that you have taught them something *definite* and *interesting*.

12. Give a brief explanation of your system for marking notebooks and grading papers. Tell them when tests will come, and so forth. Explain that these are efforts you make to help them succeed.

13. *Smile!* Keep your voice and manner pleasant. Let your students know that you are pleased to meet them and that the prospect of teaching them is a pleasure. *And be sincere about it!*

14. Watch your time! In order to get all this done, it may be helpful to have everything scheduled. Thus:

| | |
|---|---:|
| Making out seating slips: | 10 minutes |
| Giving out books, collecting receipts: | 8 minutes |
| Distributing assignment sheets, motivating students and giving first assignment: | 5 minutes |
| Necessary seat changes: | 5 minutes |
| Class discussion of the unique contribution of your subject which sets it apart and makes it important to them. (Of course seven minutes is not much time, but it is about all you can take on the first day. In succeeding lessons you will have opportunity to develop the importance of your subject to them to a fuller extent.): | 7 minutes |
| Class discussion on assigned topic for homework. Pose some provocative questions. Be sure to include non-volunteers. It creates a feeling of belonging and adds to the consciousness of being held responsible for participation in the lesson: | 3 minutes |
| Brief explanation of your marking system, when you collect notebooks, when tests come, and so forth: | 2 minutes |
| *Length of period:* | 40 minutes |

This is a tight schedule, but you can see that on the very first day it may help you to accomplish a great deal in organizing your class. Usually this will impress your students, and first impressions are especially important to adolescents.

And so, you are off to an efficient and pleasant relationship with your class.

*2. Day-by-day development of class control, one of the foundations for successful teaching. The importance of motivation in obtaining class control. Six suggestions for guidance toward class control.*

We should learn in school work, as in life, to put the most important matters first. It sounds simple, but it is often not at all easy, either to perceive or accomplish. Class control falls into this category. Frequently the beginning teacher is imbued with the idea of teaching his particular subject to a group of adolescents who will listen, bug-eyed, to his every word. If an English teacher, he dreams of teaching *Macbeth* or *Hamlet*. If a chemistry teacher, he is eager to explain the *Periodic Table* or *Formulas of Common Organic Compounds*. But whatever your subject matter, you should use it as a platform to establish class control. A measure of *surface* control is necessary to even start teaching and learning, but *real* control is the product of meaningful curriculum and teaching. Thus, avoid the implication, "Students, you behave or I won't teach and you won't learn." Such an attitude gives little attention to the nature of the learning experience or the personal significance of it to your students. To be sure, much behavior is not related to curriculum and teaching—but many of our serious problems in control are rebellions against nonsignificant learning, as students see it.

Thus one of the ways that a good teacher usually has control of his class is *through effective motivating* of his subject. This means engendering a desire to learn the subject because of an aroused interest *by the student*. Of the many factors that go into making a successful career in teaching, proper motivating of the students is generally recognized as one that is very important. Possibly more beginning teachers stumble on providing a strong motivation to learn—and consequently invite control problems—than on any other step in attaining class control. As a result, beginning teachers who neglect proper motivation sometimes find their students not paying attention to the lesson. It is helpful to keep in mind that a lack of control is a symptom rather than a cause and that poor class control frequently evolves from either improper or insufficient motivation. Whatever your subject matter, it should have strong motivation to build up student interest. In brief, *find ways to stimulate your students so that they will want to learn your subject.*

However, with a typical load of 150–180 students, it is hardly realistic that *every* student will be *completely* motivated to learn your subject. Indeed, there may be some youngsters who enter your class with an obstinate and obvious dislike for your subject. These difficult-to-motivate teen-agers we shall deal with in some detail later on. And of course there is the possibility that some motivation and subsequent interest gets lost along the way. For this reason, it is commonly advisable that you frequently rejuvenate interest with fresh motivation. To repeat once more because it is so very important: One of the ways a good teacher gains control of his class is through his students' desire to learn his subject.

Good control, you should realize, is not evidenced by a class sitting in painful silence but by the class actively engaged in a learning situation.

Admittedly some schools are more difficult to teach in than others. Also, classes within a given school may contrast sharply both in ability and conduct. Thus *where you teach and whom you teach are important factors and you should take them into consideration.* The select suburban school composed largely of the sons and daughters of successful business and professional people is likely to differ considerably from some of the large schools in the difficult areas of big cities.

Most good teachers plan motivational material to be used *as soon as possible* (usually the first day): a demonstration (science), an amusing or dramatic selection (English), an intriguing mathematical problem, and so forth, to help create *an abiding interest.* It may help if you keep in mind that one of the most effective forms of control stems from *immediate* interest. Thus, strive to make motivation an inherent part of *every* lesson and assignment.

In addition, we should remind ourselves that the concept of good class control may vary a great deal with each teacher's personality. Your fellow teachers and you are individuals with possibly very different psychological approaches. Therefore, it is rather to be expected that your reactions to a given class situation may not be the same as theirs in every respect. Indeed, there may be opposite responses. This does not necessarily mean that one is entirely right and the other entirely wrong. Because of the variation in types of classes and teacher personalities, *critical self-examination may be the key to a difficult situation in class control.*

Another factor important in class control that you should not forget is that many students need individual, *personal* encouragement and guidance for one reason or another. Some have an excessive demand upon their time by school activities. Some are poorly dressed and ill-fed. Some work long hours after school. These and other hardships may lead directly to the problem of underachievement.

Underachievement is prevalent, and it is generally recognized that frequently its roots are in emotional problems. In the case of many such students, the beginning teacher should realize that one of his most effective means of control is an understanding heart. Some students can't put effort into their school work because they are in love. Their thoughts are rosy daydreams filled with emotional situations that take every moment. Sometimes there is an ingrained sense of inferiority, and the teen-ager is convinced there is no use in even trying. Not uncommon is the youngster who feels nobody cares so why should he bother. Indeed, his family may not be concerned about his success at all. There are instances where a student challenges authority, certain that his reasoning is better than those around him who don't really know his needs. There is the possibility that a youngster actually wants to fail because of a steadily mounting pressure on him that he do better and better until he feels pushed beyond his ability. Of common occurrence is the adolescent who hides bitter antagonism behind a barrier of quiet determination to go his own way. These are examples of where the teacher needs to exercise compassion and the touch of warm, yet skillful, handling. Beginning teachers sometimes do not realize that one of their *most important functions is to understand the youngster.* Thus close contact with the guidance counselor may be very helpful. Although we have emphasized the significance of motivation in arousing your student's desire to learn, keep in mind that the boy or girl *as a person* should have an important place in your consideration. It frequently happens that knowing a teen-ager as a person gives you a lever to stimulate his interest in your subject. Indeed, when you reach into the individual student, you are usually on the path to good class control.

Thus, in working toward class control, an obvious but important fact to realize is that a class is composed of individuals. The inexperienced teacher frequently forgets this in his efforts to put across a lesson. Sometimes a beginner proceeds through his prepared material in a cut-and-dried manner that makes no allowances for the personalities in his class. In his eagerness to present specifics, he withers a youngster's interest and dulls the sparkle of enthusiasm. *Don't be afraid to be human. Avoid a cold approach.* This book is filled with hundreds of suggestions to help you become a successful teacher, but there is no substitute for the genial, friendly approach that sees John and Mary as teen-agers who are at once bold and shy, independent but conscious of their insecurity. In other words, you are dealing with young *persons*, not with the eighth period class in Room 301. And your overall aim is not only for them to master your subject, but also for you to be one of those who guide these youngsters through adolescence into achieving the threshold of young adulthood with their potentials matured to the best of your ability.

Accordingly, although the concrete suggestions that follow have an immediate application in helping you obtain class control, they are actually the means toward a larger attainment. You will probably find them useful tools toward achieving class control so that you will not become apprehensive and afraid to be the understanding leader that teen-agers need.

As you consider the various suggestions that follow this paragraph, bear in mind that they are some of the means that can possibly help you establish a good learning situation for your students. The inexperienced teacher is likely to underestimate the importance of a proper atmosphere for assisting youngsters to participate actively in lively discussions or show enthusiasm for broadening their interests in their studies. Thus, by no means should these suggestions be used in a way that would alienate students. *Develop a sense of perspective.* Keep in focus that each teen-ager is important in his own right as a young person soon to take his place in adult society. You are **NOT** privileged to be nasty-tongued, ill-mannered, and deliberately mean to a youngster because you are in a position of authority. At times you may need to correct your students, but don't shout ugly invectives. Sometimes you may be forced to administer disciplinary measures, but *never with rancor.* You are dealing with teen-agers, and at times a determined approach for proper conduct may be necessary, but don't forget that your goal is to help them achieve success in their preparation for adult life. You should establish good class control, but learn the knack of doing so *pleasantly, yet effectively.* Let your students know that you are a gentleman or a lady but that *you are firm in your intention of establishing an atmosphere conducive to learning.* Such firmness is one of the marks of a good teacher. Toward that end, here are some suggestions to help you:

1. Train your eyes to be alert. Many secondary schools have classroom doors with a glass panel for observation by a supervisor. As you walk through the halls in your free period, notice which teachers have classes that are paying attention to what is going on. That didn't "just happen." Make a point of talking either before or after school to the teachers you observed who had excellent class control. Ask them how they do it. Don't be bashful. As a beginner, you need help and they are almost invariably willing to offer suggestions. You may be amazed at the variety of methods different teachers have. Try them out on your classes. Some of them you probably will naturally reject; others may fit your personality and your classes' needs and become immediately effective. Thus, it seems obvious that techniques which appeal to a dynamic type of teacher may not be successful with a person who has a gentle outlook on life. Also, sometimes techniques that may be highly effective with a class of gifted students may fail in dealing with a retarded group.

2. Have conferences with your subject supervisor. Suggestions offered by him may be especially worthwhile. To begin with, it is customarily his duty to observe and make reports on

the teachers in his department. Thus he nearly always has the advantage of a many-sided viewpoint. In addition, as indicated by his position, he is usually a superior teacher himself. Furthermore, he is commonly eager to have you an effective member of his department. Thus he will often be of possible help in giving you suggestions from his own experience.

3. Consult the supervisor in charge of discipline. He is normally in a position to give you authoritative advice on special discipline problems in your school.

4. Purchase a small spiral notebook that can be slipped into your handbag or pocket. Use this notebook constantly for "Class Control Suggestions" as you come across them. If you persist in its use, you may possibly find it an invaluable aid.

5. Arrange for observation of good teachers. Some schools use a buddy system where an experienced, friendly teacher volunteers to help a beginner. Also, the supervisor of your subject usually prizes the teacher who has good control of his classes. Ask your subject supervisor whom he considers to be some of the best teachers in his department and for permission to observe them teaching. Talk to these teachers. Ask them for the methods they use to establish control. If possible, make an appointment to observe each one teach a class. Note how control is established. The observation of expert teachers is sometimes of inestimable value at the start of your career. Unfortunately many beginning teachers tend to take a dim view of observing others whether from arrogance, timidity, or failure to recognize its importance. After you have made only a few observations, you will probably become conscious of their importance in learning teaching techniques and the establishment of control in a class. Of possibly even more value than observation alone, is for you to get a superior teacher to analyze his teaching: why it is effective and what you might incorporate into your lessons.

6. Be prepared to take notes of worthwhile items whenever class-control procedures are discussed at faculty or department conferences. Because class control in some schools is such an important topic, it may be frequently presented either in the form of specific problems or as established procedures. The discussions at these conferences often prove helpful.

In other words, it is generally advisable to take advan-

tage of the wealth of experience that is in your school. Of course
you usually find some persons more cooperative than others. That
is to be expected. But commonly the old-timer is more than willing
to extend a helping hand.

### 3. The challenge of academically gifted students.

We have already stressed that specific suggestions made throughout this book should be adjusted to the actual classes you face in
your particular school and to your own personality. If you are a
teacher starting your career in a difficult area of a large city
school having youngsters hard to control, you may find helpful
some special advice that will be given later in this chapter. If you
are beginning in an average school with classes of a middle-type
behavior, your problems are usually easier to solve. Suggestions
for some of the typical average-school problems follow as the
next topic. If your classes are composed of gifted students—frequently found in select suburban schools—there is a special challenge. For example, if there is one group that does not seem to
need an overemphasis on behavioral control, it would seem to be
the academically gifted students. In this case class control, too
enthusiastically applied, might be hindering some other instructional goals such as the development of originality or productive
thinking. For gifted students there is a need for freedom, always
of course under supervision, to explore and to work on their own.
The challenge is for you to develop their potentials and special
abilities. The whole nature of independent study is one of the
most frequent recommendations in programs for gifted students.

### 4. Seven helpful suggestions for the average school.

There is usually considerable variation in classes even in an
average school, especially if it is a large one. Here are some suggestions that may prove helpful if you are beginning your teaching career in the average type of school. Remember that your

personality, training, and educational philosophy are important factors. In addition, you should understand that the advice given in this handbook cannot cover all possible situations because secondary schools differ widely across the nation. Advice which fits neatly into one situation may not be applicable in another. In general, therefore, you should carefully evaluate and modify in order to meet the demands of your particular situation. To put it another way, keep in mind that the suggestions in this handbook are intended as helpful guidelines. Their use depends very largely upon your need for them as the occasion arises in your particular school or classroom. The suggestions are:

1. Strive to have your students pay attention to the lesson. Sometimes this is difficult to achieve, but it is generally accepted as promoting effective learning. But don't demand 100 percent attention at all times. If you do, you are expecting something that no human being is capable of, whether a child or an adult. Some allowance must be made for the fact that all human beings fall short of perfection. Indeed, 100 percent attention does not automatically insure 100 percent learning. But an attentive class is nearly always more responsive to its lesson. Thus, as a general rule, you should not permit a student to read a newspaper or magazine, draw pictures, scribble doodles, do a crossword puzzle, or hold a personal conversation with his neighbor when he is supposed to be taking part in the lesson. Many teachers prefer a relaxed buzz to start a lesson—let the students settle down—and if the students know that when the teacher starts talking, he is bound to say something intriguing, there is no problem in getting and holding attention. In fact, in select suburban schools it may well be argued that there is considerable latitude in the need for a student to pay attention every minute. On the other hand, in some of the more difficult schools with large, unruly classes, it may be advisable to work steadily toward having close attention from the very beginning of the period.

2. Try to have each youngster be courteous to the student making a contribution to the lesson. This usually engenders a spirit of cooperation. If a youngster is deliberately ignoring the speaker, hold up your hand, stop the discussion, and say, "Just a moment, Ethel (the person speaking), we have an interruption.

I am sorry. What is your problem, Charles (the person who turned around to hold a personal conversation with his neighbor)? May I help you?" If necessary, let Charles know he has been rude to Ethel and the rest of the class that was paying attention. *Be kind, but firm.* Explain that you expect courtesy from one member of the class to another. Follow exactly the same procedure each time there is an obvious lack of cooperation. *For the first few days of the term concentrate on this procedure. It is of more importance than any discussion.* Usually by the end of the first week, your students realize that they should be polite to one another when a contribution is being made to the lesson. Learn to use courtesy to build cooperation and class respect. As a general rule, you will find it a helpful step for good class control.

3. Strangely enough, the first five minutes are usually of more importance in establishing class control than the other thirty-five. (Secondary school periods are typically 40 to 55 minutes in length.) The beginning of the period is normally extremely significant. It defines your approach to the whole problem of control. Consequently, *control should be in evidence from the moment a student enters your room,* but not through a prisonlike atmosphere. You and your room should reflect warmth and an invitation to learning. Encourage your students to look at a lively bulletin board that is kept up-to-date with interesting daily changes apropos of the lesson. However, if you permit students to walk around aimlessly and be boisterous until the bell rings, you've usually begun your lesson with a handicap. This is one of the commonest mistakes made by beginning teachers. After students have seen the bulletin board, it is generally advisable to insist that they go directly to their seats. Another helpful suggestion is to establish a three- or four-minute period for students to study their notes before the class begins. Thus all students will be in their seats quietly studying when the bell rings for the beginning of the lesson. Such a system constructs a sense of individual and class control that is truly remarkable. In addition to the beginning of the period, *transitions from one type of activity to another are frequently critical points in a lesson.*

4. It is seldom advisable to permit yourself to become embroiled in an argument with a student in front of your class.

To begin with, it is usually belittling to your dignity, and your image as the leader of the class will frequently suffer. Strive to retain your personal dignity. Always be a lady or a gentleman, even when under considerable provocation. Your class will almost always admire you for it.

5. What punishment should be given to a student who disrupts your control? There is no hard-and-fast rule. Each situation must be evaluated for itself. You will usually find it generally helpful to follow this advice: Give *immediate* rather than severe punishment. Opinions vary tremendously as to what is effective and proper. Some teachers are convinced that writing "sentences" is more punishment than detention. For example, "I must not throw chalk in the classroom" written one hundred times will be confining on students with other commitments—especially if on a team or in a school play. Other teachers feel that writing such a sentence a number of times serves no real purpose. They feel it would be better to have the student report after school when you could discuss the matter of his misconduct in detail and suggest ways of making an improvement. If he has a job after school, give him permission to come before school. If you do have detention, keep a careful record of each infraction that he makes so that you are not relying upon memory and he knows that you are being honest with him. If the student fails to report, double his time say some teachers. If he persists and days go by, take the matter up with your subject supervisor or the supervisor in charge of discipline. However, think through this matter of detention carefully. Many teachers today have given up on detention, especially doubling of time, although some find it very effective. But certainly detention is not suitable punishment for *every* type of offense. Ideally, the punishment should fit the infraction. Also, commonly aim to *make the punishment as light as possible and yet corrective in principle*. Indeed, to be effective punishment should achieve correction and develop the right attitude in the student. Thus, note that sometimes a student may actually get satisfaction out of detention! Of course you should be certain that a student deserves punishment. Listen to his story *carefully, patiently, and sympathetically;* avoid the slightest tinge of harsh, ruthless treatment. Remember, the aver-

age adolescent doesn't mind deserved punishment, but he resents unfairness. On the other hand, avoid permitting a student to escape *deserved* punishment. In this connection, be sure that you are able to enforce the punishment. Most experienced teachers are agreed on another basic point: follow the general rule that there is no favoritism. One more suggestion is that perhaps you might find a conference with the student's guidance counselor helpful. If serious trouble is indicated, it may be advisable to confer with the discipline supervisor. You may find this suggestion helpful: notify the parents. A case does not have to be extreme to write to them. Some young teachers establish early relations with parents by telephoning them—a most effective method. Very seldom do you find parents who are not cooperative in the matter of discipline. Thus your approach should be carefully designed so that you help the youngster yet you do not build resentment against yourself and your subject. Generally speaking, rarely punish a whole class for the misconduct of an individual. And of course avoid giving an increased assignment as punishment because it is better that punishment not be associated with your subject material.

6. What attitude should you have to develop good class control? As emphasized previously, the type of school you are in and your personality are two important factors that should be blended for effective control. What would succeed in the superior school educating gifted children may not be effective in a difficult urban school composed of classes where the youngsters sometimes are inclined to be disorderly and may need to be under strong control. In many of our average schools, formality is often unnecessary and may get in the way of the learning process. The basic approach is to strive for each student to share in the lesson. Active participation—through motivation to learn and personal rapport—tends to eliminate control problems. It is helpful to take the attitude that each student is expected to make his contribution toward developing the lesson.

7. As a general rule, make every effort to be in your room before the class arrives. This can become difficult if you have to go from one end of the building to the other or from the first to the fourth floor. If you travel a long distance between

classes, usually make sure that you are ready to leave the last classroom as soon as the bell rings for the end of the period. Frequently, beginning teachers chat overlong with students about the lesson or dally along the way and arrive late at their next class. Thus they may be faced with a control problem that could have been avoided. Under ordinary circumstances you should be able to get to your class to see that control is established from the start of the period and it is generally advisable to do so.

As you are probably aware, some of these suggestions are highly dependent upon the specific class to which they would apply. As previously pointed out, what would be possibly of value to beginning teachers who are entering some of the very large schools might not apply to small suburban schools, where a very different relationship with students is set up, even though both could be classified as average schools. Thus it is possible that some schools may employ successful procedures that contrast with equally successful procedures in other schools. You should allow for local differences that are almost certain to arise.

### 5. Eight suggestions for unruly classes in difficult schools where control is a major problem.

It may be that your appointment is to a city school in a district where rigid control is required. In such a case you may find it necessary to acquaint yourself with the realities of the situation so that you can teach there effectively.

The suggestions that follow this paragraph are specifically designed to help you if you are beginning in a school where control is a major problem. Do not feel, as a result of reading these suggestions, that you are sitting on a seething volcano, and that teaching in a difficult school is necessarily a nerve-wracking job—indeed not, if you have the proper approach. In fact, teaching in a deprived-area school can be extremely rewarding. You are frequently in a position to do a great service to many teen-agers. In an underprivileged neighborhood you may

well be one of your students' few contacts with culture, refine-
ment, and a hope for the future. Meeting this challenge can
make your lifework in education *very* meaningful. A good teacher
in one of these schools can put stars in the eyes of his students,
and this makes all the difference in the world. The pleasure and
worthiness derived from such a contact, however, normally requires a sure-footed approach. It is generally helpful to have a
knowledge of what to do if a difficult situation develops. Of
course in some difficult schools control problems are more likely
to occur than in others. If your beginning experience is in a
large city where you have been given extremely unruly classes,
you may find the following suggestions of further assistance:

    1. How strict must you be with extremely unruly
classes? In a school with hard-to-control classes, you commonly
need to be definitely positive, but **DO NOT DEVELOP A PUNITIVE
APPROACH.** It may help you to keep this thought in mind: *Be
friendly, but firm.* Say what you mean and mean what you say.
You can get class control by adopting the both-a-leader-and-a-
friend attitude. However, rarely overlook deliberate disobedience.
Frankly, as a beginner in a difficult school you will usually find
it helpful to be assertive in your control. Make it a general rule
that you seldom allow leeway when it comes to control. The first
two weeks in particular strive for every student's cooperation.
Most beginning teachers have a yearning to be liked by their
students, and this is understandable, but don't purchase their
admiration at the expense of the class's welfare. In general don't
use the soft-glove treatment when faced with a teen-ager's deliberate misconduct. In this connection, however, it must be
clearly understood that control is *not* to be purchased by being
sarcastic and nasty. *An ugly attitude should never be exhibited
to any student at any time.* You should be positive, however, and
determined to establish complete control. In these classes, good
management requires an unqualified stability in handling unruly
teen-agers. With difficult youngsters it is better to nip trouble
in the bud than to wait until it blossoms into a major problem.

    2. Be *sincere* in your efforts to help students in a diffi-
cult class. The gifted student in a select suburban school usually
has the advantage of capable parents and an excellent environ-

ment. In the deprived neighborhood, you may be the only source of encouragement and inspiration. Keep alert for every opportunity to help the hard-to-control—not by being a namby-pamby, but by demanding the best work and conduct you can get from them. They have had too many years of school to be lured by a casual, unrealistic approach. The unruly students typically know the teacher who will enforce control and the one who won't. Unfortunately, once you lose control of classes difficult to handle, it is usually almost impossible to get it back again. Therefore, to repeat, be sincere and keep alert. At the slightest evidence of a disorderly teen-ager's attempt to disorganize your class, assume a stern aspect. If necessary, get your temper up! Of course your manner should be more apparent than real. Learn to act the necessary part. However, a teacher who actually becomes upset or angry loses his ability to cope with situations and can be baited into outbursts by troublemakers. Keep insisting that every student makes a contribution to the lesson. Generally speaking, give special attention to any youngster who doesn't try to participate. Let such a student know that *you* are working to the best of *your* ability for *everyone* to pass your subject. *And mean it!* Furthermore, you insist that everyone get the highest grade possible with *his* potential. Unfortunately some beginning teachers make the mistake of threatening a difficult-to-control youngster with failure unless he behaves. As a rule it is better to make your approach positive and assuring. Strangely enough, the students will usually respect you for your attitude. It marks you as a person sincerely dedicated to helping them, and that is really what they want. Show them that you have an affectionate regard for them—you'll enjoy a laugh with them— but you expect response to control. One caution may be necessary: New teachers are sometimes so insecure that they put on a tough front which is patently false and needlessly antagonize their students. In other words, they abuse their authority. If a class *as a whole* disapproves of your actions, check carefully on yourself. Sometimes it is not *what* we do, but the *way* we do it that is bad.

3. It is usually not advisable to turn your back on an unruly class. In particular, a beginning teacher should avoid

doing so. It's too much of a temptation to too many. At such a moment, in some classes with poor conduct, students difficult to control may throw chalk, clips, and paper airplanes across the room. One suggestion is that when you use the chalkboard, write a few words at a time and keep glancing at the class. Still better, turn partially so that you constantly keep an eye on the students who tend to be uncooperative. Perhaps you feel this is an exaggeration, but it isn't in difficult schools. In fact, in some problem schools, it is frequently imperative. As a general rule, keep your eyes on a class prone to misconduct until you have established a pleasant but firm control.

4. Be extremely careful not to make false accusations of misconduct. A beginning teacher, desperately striving to maintain control over an unruly class, may lash out at a student without being absolutely sure of his guilt. Under these circumstances, the beginning teacher often hears a defense something like this: "Who me? *I* didn't do a thing. Not me. Ask anyone. He'll tell you. Why are you picking on *me*? Gee!" And then his buddy will add his fuel to the fire. "Yeah. The teacher's unfair. Always picking on someone." This may bring the entire class down on you. As a matter of policy, think carefully before you make an accusation. For this group in particular, you should have definite proof.

5. To paraphrase a quotation, a class is as strong as its weakest member. This is doubly so when it comes to establishing control in difficult classes. As a general rule, any deliberate infraction should be noted and a record made, even if only a check mark. The class takes its cue from its teacher. If you overlook an obvious infraction, you can hardly expect the class to take your control seriously. Keeping a record gives positive evidence to an unruly teen-ager that you are concerned about him when he is not behaving. Be kind and understanding, but positive on your insistence that he must do his share in putting the welfare of the class first.

6. Be extra firm in requesting every student to participate in the lesson and to respect another student's contribution. One suggestion is to have a direct follow-up on the student who interrupted the lesson by his misconduct, calling upon him to

evaluate the contribution. Both he and the class will understand that you are checking on his taking part in the lesson. The fact that the checking is immediate makes it doubly effective. Sometimes it may be advisable to stress repeatedly that anyone interrupting a discussion with misconduct can be expected to give an evaluation and be graded accordingly.

7. Make a list of students who are inattentive for each class. Strive to get them into the class discussion of the lesson and carry their share of the load of contributions. To repeat, impress upon each student that it is to his benefit to pay close attention to the lesson and *that he owes himself the best marks he can get.* Have a direct follow-up program. This pinpoints each student to do his utmost. For example, emphasize in private conference at the end of the period why you want him to participate. Explain that a discussion should be a rewarding experience for *everyone* in the class. In most cases he will understand and appreciate your trying to help him. The fact that your follow-up is immediate usually makes it very effective. In very difficult classes it may be worthwhile to use this procedure constantly. Sometimes a beginning teacher doesn't fully realize that a class is composed of individuals, and this is an important factor in establishing control. To put it another way, *control over each individual gives you control over the class.*

8. Strive to remain calm and confident. Aim for the sure, firm—yet pleasant—touch with unruly teen-agers. A beginning teacher frequently makes one of two errors: First, he may ignore the misconduct of a class, even to the extent of permitting pandemonium. He proceeds with the lesson, struggling to make himself heard although few if any of the youngsters are paying attention to him. Second, he may shout for order at the slightest threat to his control. As a consequence he frequently builds up an atmosphere of deep antagonism. The key to dealing with difficult-to-control teen-agers is to let them know that along with being concerned for their welfare, you expect positive cooperation. In general, laugh and smile when the occasion is suitable. Demonstrate that you enjoy being with them, but you don't intend to put up with any nonsense. They have to understand that there are boundaries to what is permitted and

they must learn to control themselves. It is natural for a young teacher starting in a difficult school to feel a certain amount of tension. But as the days, weeks, and months roll by, you will characteristically become ever more competent and confident of your ability. Take the long-range view that what you do to help these teen-agers achieve a full measure of maturity is very worthwhile.

It is possible that the advice dealing with difficult schools and unruly classes given on these pages may appear very scary to a beginning teacher. Perhaps you may get the impression that teen-agers prone to misconduct are bound to take advantage of you. This is not at all necessarily or even probably true. But it is wise to be prepared when one walks into a difficult situation. The student in underprivileged and problem areas is especially appreciative of a teacher who is genuinely concerned about his pupils. Frequently the most rewarding classes in terms of student appreciation and personal accomplishment are found with the students who have limited opportunities. *When they realize that you are sincerely dedicated to helping them, but that you will tolerate no disorder, control problems largely disappear.* Putting it another way, it is commonly felt that it is your inherent interest in the youngsters themselves that makes for successful teaching—not rules on when and how to teach what—although these serve their purpose. Indeed, some highly disorganized teachers who manage to get their message of devotion and accomplishment to their difficult students may be inspired teachers who achieve a measure of greatness.

*6. Class control those first ten days in the superior, average, and difficult schools.*

It is usually true that in the select superior school the beginning teacher is greeted with enthusiasm by his students. Although a degree of control is necessary, the academically gifted student generally has a respectful attitude. As a result there is a minimal need for emphasis on proper conduct. From the very start of the class, your emphasis should be on original thinking and self-motivation toward productive scholarship.

In the average school your classes usually hand you priceless cooperation the first two weeks. They are sizing you up, waiting for you to establish your standards. They want to know what you are like. If you are a newcomer to the school, they know it. Even if they are freshmen, the word spreads fast. If you have advanced students, they have you pegged for a beginner as soon as they see you. They are all ears for the first cues that will reveal your weaknesses and strengths. For these ten days you have them in the palm of your hand. They are yours to do with as you choose so far as control is concerned. And what kind of class control you have is one of the labels they are going to stick on you. They are watching your every move when the matter of control comes up. And it will, you can be sure of that. So get yourself set to hold onto the cooperation they bring you when they are evaluating you during those first two weeks. Stress tact and diplomacy, but get tough if by chance an occasion should demand it. But as a general rule, in the average school there is no need to be overly concerned about control. On the opening day your classes pay careful attention. There is usually no problem with control. They want to make a good impression. When you call for order, they are instantly quiet. As the weeks roll on, keep this warm, friendly feeling between you and your classes, but always with firm control in evidence when a situation seems to slip out of hand.

If you are entering one of the difficult schools struggling with large classes and a high percentage of pupils who need strong behavioral control, keep a tight rein on each class for the first ten days. Of course you must employ the highest level of guidance to which your students will respond. If they react only to negative motivation, then such must be used until you can assist them into good control through a desire to learn your subject. Classroom situations in some of our nation's disadvantaged areas necessitate practices that may be frowned upon in other areas. For example, in some instances you may find that your youngsters are deliberately testing you as to your ability to hold them in line. In other words, they may be waiting to see if you are capable of controlling them. Sometimes it's that simple, especially if you are in an extremely difficult school with very unruly classes. If you are slack in maintaining order, they may laugh and howl at nothing, deliberately creating a disturbance. The bolder ones in such a class may pull every trick in the bag to make the situation as bad as possible. More than one beginning teacher in such a school has found the unruly class out of control the graveyard of his professional dreams. Therefore, if you are handling youngsters of this type, it may be advisable to look and listen for signs of disorder. Make it a rule to be alert. Generally speaking, there's danger ahead if you get careless with your control of troublesome teen-agers in difficult classes. It may be helpful to remember this advice: Don't worry about the amount of subject material covered the first two weeks. A small amount of content taught thoroughly with excellent control maintained at all times is your goal with a group that tends to be disorderly. Develop a strong attitude of *preventive* class control. These youngsters have to learn where and what the limits of permissibility are, and that punishment sometimes has to be employed to help them learn what these limits are. Of course setting such limits requires both firmness and perseverance. On occasion you may be forced to act on the basis of expediency, but still do your best to apply what you know about adolescent growth and development.

When you have trained your classes for good control, you can cover the material from your syllabus without difficulty, and these youngsters will be a pleasure to teach.


*7. It is usually helpful to have definite classroom procedure. Eight steps that will assist control for the beginning teacher.*


You may find it helpful to write out a schedule of what your procedure will be from the very start of the period. This schedule is not in reference to your lesson plan which covers the content and manner of presentation of subject material. What you should have in mind here is the organizational steps you are going to take, for example:

1. Stand in the doorway of your room. If the principal requests that you be in the hallway during the passing of classes, then stand so that you can keep an eye turned into your room.

2. Nod a greeting to each student as he enters your room, but don't greet him effusively. Be businesslike. We shall speak more about the importance of this later.

3. Strive to be inside your door as soon as the bell rings for commencing the period. As mentioned previously, if possible get inside before then. Generally speaking, the sooner, the better.

4. After looking at the daily bulletin board, is everyone in his seat?

5. Has every student opened his notebook?

a. Is he studying the lesson for the day?
b. Is he reviewing yesterday's work?

6. The moment the bell rings, hand quiz papers (3 by 6) to students to distribute.

7. Ask at least one question on review and at least one on that day's lesson.

8. Collect quiz papers. They should be rated and returned the next day as an incentive to further work.

Usually effective, yet simple, this suggested routine for starting each class may be a decided help. As a rule it means that you are now ready for your formal lesson plan for that day and a controlled atmosphere normally has been established.

*Of course the opening device given is but an example of many that may be used.* The technique employed of giving a daily quiz is frowned upon by some teachers who feel that it suggests that the main reason to learn is to answer quiz questions correctly. Those in favor of the daily quiz feel that it builds up confidence in the students that they are mastering the work as it progresses and that it enables the teacher to help promptly any students who obviously don't understand. In addition, the daily quiz serves as a deterrent for some students who might otherwise skip their preparation for the lesson.

*8. Permission to leave the room. Procedure in the superior and average schools. Its subtle threat to control in difficult schools. Eleven suggestions for use in unruly classes.*

In a superior school generally there is no need for a student to ask for permission to leave the room to use the lavatory. The philosophy in the superior school is that an adolescent is to be treated like a responsible adult who knows when to leave the room and the proper conduct for doing so. In the superior school the student is not likely to abuse this privilege. The student is expected to go and return without any problem whatsoever and no hall pass is required.

The average school on the other hand usually exercises a moderate amount of control. The student may ask the teacher for the pass and he quietly leaves the room. Or, the pass may be located in a convenient place where all he has to do is pick it up and go. The pass serves as a means of identification as to the room he is coming from in the event that some special need should arise. When he returns he quietly takes his seat and there is no disturbance of the class.

It is possible, however, that in a difficult school in a problem area such as in some of our large cities, the granting of permission to leave the room may be a factor in class control, especially for a beginning teacher. It is understood that the pass for a student to go to the lavatory is to be given if it is needed. But how are you to know when it is a legitimate request? This is the angle that some unruly students may use against a beginning teacher. You may find that the period has scarcely started when someone asks for the pass. You give it to him. Immediately another hand goes up. "May I have it when he returns?" This is frequently accompanied by a painful grimace to impress you. You say, "Yes." Possibly the situation expands. Another hand goes up. "I'm next." Someone laughs. You think this is an exaggeration? Not at all if your class is a difficult one. In a few minutes (we hope!) the person with the pass returns. Three more hands go up. They might as well get into the act. The second person jumps up for the pass. You protest. "But you promised. Remember?" You weakly nod and hand it to him. By this time the entire class is waiting for the second customer to return and watching to see who will get the pass next. The parade is on. It has become a game. Admittedly the attention of the class is not on the lesson.

And here is another suggestion for the beginning teacher handling classes prone to misconduct: Think twice before you give the pass to an unruly youngster with the idea that this gets him out of your hair, or that it will bribe him into behaving when he returns. The class will quickly catch on and correctly label you a weakling. In classes of this type control should be obtained and maintained by being sincere with your students, yet having a positive and realistic attitude. Here are some suggestions that you may find of help in controlling the pass situation if you find yourself in serious trouble in this respect:

1. Keep a record of anyone getting the pass. Have a notebook for this purpose. Have student sign his name. You check the time and watch him write it down. He will also put down the time when he returns, and again you check that it is correct. Incidentally, this record serves a double purpose. Occasionally the discipline supervisor wishes to track down students who were out of the classrooms when some mischief was done. Your record will be of definite assistance.

2. Impress upon the student that he has a limited time to be out of the room because he is missing part of his lesson. Consequently, you are limiting him to ten minutes.

3. Make him realize that the pass cannot be given frequently to any one student. Explain that there are thirty-five other members in the class and they have to be considered. He will usually understand and the class will generally approve. If there is a genuine need for the pass, of course you should give it to him, but constantly discourage the fakers.

4. Seldom give the pass at the beginning of the period unless it is a matter of obvious emergency. Just say, "Sorry, you

had your opportunity a few minutes ago. Your class is now in session."

5. In the middle of the period ask him to wait a few minutes. This serves as a test for authenticity. The probability is that he won't ask again, if you've made it evident you don't approve of his missing part of his lesson. If he does ask again, it is apt to be a genuine need.

6. Toward the end of the period, tell him to wait a couple of minutes and the period will be over.

7. Whenever a student returns from the lavatory reeking of cigarette smoke, make a note. This is undoubtedly his reason for asking for the pass. Let him know that you noticed and that his chances of getting the pass are dim if he is having a smoke rather than contributing to the class discussion. Explain that it is his obligation to take an active part in the lesson.

8. One of the tip-offs for genuine need is when a youngster suddenly gets up, even while someone is making a contribution to the lesson, and hurries to your desk. He may hasten out of the room without signing your pass-book. In that case, write down his name and the time yourself. The area of common sense should prevail here.

9. If a student asks for the pass and appears really ill, send another student along as a security measure. It doesn't happen often, but it does occur. Indeed, follow this procedure in any type of class, unruly or not.

10. Generally speaking, you should not give the pass out more than once or twice in the whole day. In fact, there should be many days when it is not given at all. Of course your individual judgment should be used as some schools, unfortunately, have limited lavatory facilities to allow all students to care for their bodily functions within the time permitted.

11. If a physical need exists for frequent use of the pass, it should be supported by a doctor's statement, a confirmation from the school nurse, a note from the parent, or a message from the guidance counselor.

And here we add the advice that commonly an excellent basis for good class control with teen-agers hard to handle is to *have only the rules you intend to enforce.*

Remember, there is nothing for you to be afraid of in beginning your teaching career in a difficult school. *It is merely a matter of quickly becoming adjusted to the technique for positive control.* Once you learn how to control these teen-agers pleasantly but firmly, you become a vital force in helping them achieve success in life—the reward of a good teacher.

In closing this chapter, we trust that some of these practical suggestions that come from experience may help you through your probationary period whether it is in a superior, average, or difficult school.

# CHAPTER 2
# *Introducing Your Subject*

*1. The necessity for convincing the class of the value of your subject.*

Many subjects are established as requirements by either the state or the local board of education. For example, English is universally required in secondary schools for every grade level. Also, American history is customarily required as well as world history. For academic diplomas a certain amount of mathematics, science, and a language are usually needed. It is true that today a student has electives he was not permitted years ago. But even if he selects a subject himself, a student may not realize its full value. Thus, whether the subject is required or elected, the student should be made aware of its importance *to him.*

Isn't it true that values are relative? What is of extreme need to another person may be of little or no concern to you. And what is of urgency today, by next year may be forgotten. Thus, it is a mistake for any teacher to assume that his students will automatically realize the importance of the subjects he is teaching. Of course we are not referring to the motivating of students for a unit of study. That will be taken care of in your lesson plans. But as a beginning teacher, in particular, make a point of *repeatedly* emphasizing throughout the school year the definite values of your subject to your students. If you are not convinced of its worthwhileness, you can scarcely expect them to be.

Another factor that is usually very important in convincing your students that your subject is worthwhile is your own attitude toward it. Your enthusiasm is ordinarily reflected in your gestures, your expression, your voice. It is an intangible that permeates the classroom in a strange, yet positive manner. It is commonly true that the enthusiasm of the teacher for his subject is contagious. Isn't enthusiasm in itself inspiring?

Of course repeatedly telling the student how valuable your subject is, or your own enthusiasm, is not sufficient. *Your subject should be carefully presented so as to convince the student of its value to him.* In the end, a student's realization of the importance of any subject will typically be a summation of his experiences in it.

Do not make the error of treating your class as a captive audience. Do you expect them to sit there, hands folded, eyes straight ahead, mouths closed, while you harangue them? This is another serious error made by many beginning teachers. All that you are doing is showing off your knowledge. In order to convince the class of the value of what they are learning, *the approach should be made through the members of the class itself.* Here are suggestions:

1. The opening assignment for the first day can be, "Why is the study of this subject important in today's world?" Have each student prepare three reasons. Use this material as the basis for a class discussion the next day.

2. Another possibility is to have a debate on, "Should more time be given to the study of this subject in secondary schools today?" The pros and cons developed will serve as a stimulating platform for your enlargement.

3. On the first day that the class meets, begin a discussion by asking a question such as, "What are the advantages of taking this subject now, rather than beginning its study in college?"

The point is, whatever type of approach you use, strive to convince your class that you are enthusiastic about your subject, that it is a valuable one in the world, and that it is of personal importance to each student.

Of course the student has the pressure on him of having to pass your subject so that he can graduate. But isn't that, indeed, a miserable viewpoint? Unfortunately, it is the one that is sometimes used by some teachers. Literally it amounts to an intimidation: if you don't pass my subject you can't graduate. That may be true, but that is *not* the best approach to use. If it is a required subject, you should take the trouble to explain to your students *why* the board of education insists everyone have it. If the subject is an elective, then explain its worthwhileness in modern life.

### 2. Your best friend is your lesson plan. Types of plans. What should be included.

It is amazing how some beginning teachers in secondary schools think they can teach an effective lesson without a plan. Even teachers with many years of experience are usually careful to organize their material. In many cases failure to have a lesson plan is brought about by the fact that sometimes beginning teachers believe, inasmuch as they have been through college, that they are far superior to the secondary school student and detailed preparation isn't necessary. But that isn't the point. You should realize that you have a *definite* amount of subject material to cover in a *definite* amount of time. Furthermore, individual needs and abilities of your classes vary. Therefore, normally it is helpful to have your plan highly developed. In most instances the better you organize your lessons, the more successful they will be. For practical purposes, *a good plan is your best friend.*

In your lesson planning, be sure to stress the factor of student-learning activities. Content is important, but many students have no interest in it *unless they are involved in varied, exciting activities*. Generally speaking, change the type of lesson every day. Strive to involve the student's experiences in panels, dramatizations, class discussions, buzz sessions, and such. The fundamental principle to remember is: *Learning is essentially a do-it-yourself project*. Keep in mind that many students are not academically inclined. Your lesson as a rule should be carefully planned if you are going to involve them in its content.

Plans vary in type according to the length of time for which they are intended. Of course a unit plan is based upon the nature of the unit rather than a certain number of days. The following are three basic guides:

1. You ordinarily need a daily lesson plan. This is written in detail and intended to cover in a thorough manner the topic assigned for that day. It should include a motivation factor to arouse the student's interest. Opinions vary as to what is the most effective format. Sometimes supervisors are insistent that you follow a specific pattern. In other cases supervisors are lenient so long as you have a definite written plan that they can inspect at any time they choose. Some of the benefits of a daily plan are as follows:

a. Establishes a definite goal for that lesson.
b. Organizes the material for full development and proper sequence.
c. Serves as a platform for trying different techniques.
d. Gives you confidence.

2. You should have a weekly plan. Usually this does not have to be in detail, but there ought to be a clear indication of how much material will be given your class, and also the order in which it will be presented. Consequently, it is usually arranged by days in topic and subtopic form. However, some supervisors insist that weekly plans be fully written out. For one thing, weekly plans show you know where you are going. Second, these plans may be used in the event of your illness, in which case your substitute will know what ground is to be covered.

3. A term plan should be made. This is a schedule for the amount of content to be covered by the first marking period, the midterm examinations, and the final weeks of the term. Thus, in a sense you are like a railroad engineer. You have a

certain number of stops to make and you have a schedule to maintain. You are due at your destination on a definite day with a certain bulk of material covered so that your students can pass their final examinations. However, as a beginner you could expect to modify your original term plan. Different classes because of varying abilities and interests cannot maintain the same schedule. The pace of a class would influence your term plan. To start with, you could probably only sketch a term plan, but after the first month you should revise it completely into a more realistic program.

Plans should be constructed carefully. The daily lesson plan is often the center of discussion in department and faculty meetings. There are many variations in its format. In a large secondary school of some seventy-five or more teachers, probably there are no two who use exactly the same outline for a daily plan, nor develop it in exactly the same manner. There are many kinds of lessons, of course. The laboratory lesson varies widely from one in physical education. An example of a good basic plan for a formal lesson in an academic classroom is as follows:

MOTIVATION

State how you are going to interest the students in the lesson. Strive to make certain that the lesson will be related to the daily lives of teen-agers, for example, the TV programs they see and their experiences. Commonly give the topic in the form of a simple problem-question, and usually have about four or five pivotal questions leading to the aim.

AIM

State the purpose of the lesson as derived from your motivation. It should be definite. Strive to express it in the form of a problem-question.

DEVELOPMENT (first half)

In developing your lesson, connect it with previous experiences of your students if at all possible. The subject matter ought to show logical procedure. Attention should be paid to the outcomes of the lesson in terms of social growth, individual expression, and the opportunity for original thinking. Questions should be carefully worded for clarity and designed to stimulate thought and reasoning power.

### MIDSUMMARY (medial)

Quickly review the major points of the material you have gone over by asking questions. The "how" and "why" type are especially useful. (A summary may be used at any point in a lesson if you wish to check how thoroughly the students have absorbed the subject matter.) A midsummary determines that the students clearly understand the first half of the lesson. Use summaries to unify divisions of a lesson.

### DEVELOPMENT (second half)

There should be plenty of material prepared for a full lesson. It is better to have too much than not enough.

### SUMMARY (final)

Frame questions to elicit from the students all the significant parts of the lesson. Pose specific, pivotal questions. Illustrative material such as a film may be used in the summary. Include a brief test to evaluate absorption of the material.

### ASSIGNMENT

State what the students are to do for tomorrow. Make sure they copy the assignment and give sufficient guidance to help them do it. *Be sure to give the reason for the assignment. Show its importance to them: Motivating students to do the homework is very important.* One caution: a hurried assignment frequently results when given at the end of the period. Allow sufficient time, or else give the assignment at the beginning of the period.

Variations of this basic plan are found in each of its sections. For example, in some subjects the statement of the *aim* is omitted, as the assigned topic for the day may indicate the purpose of the lesson. There may be no need to write out *materials* if you use an assignment sheet or if you do not use visual aids or other equipment. Or, *motivation* might sometimes be omitted, as in geometry where the reason for studying the content doesn't necessarily vary from day to day. *Development* becomes more or less detailed according to the teacher's personal likes. A few words on a topic may suffice for some, whereas others desire elaborate notes to help them. However, beginning teachers, as mentioned previously, as a rule find it helpful to use detailed development. A *summary* is sometimes in the form of a test or film. On the other hand, some teachers use more than one midlesson (medial) summary in addition to the final summation. The *assignment* may be handled, as suggested, by separate sheets. Also, frequently it is given at the beginning of the period. Sometimes teachers hand the assignment to a student and ask him to write it on the board. But a word of caution is needed as to what can be eliminated. Your supervisor may request a definite form to be followed. And even experienced teachers have conflicting ideas. A mathematics teacher, for example, may question the elimination of motivation in geometry and, probably, *any* presentation of five minutes or more duration should be summarized.

Occasionally we meet the beginning teacher who offers an alibi for not having complete lesson plans. He forgot, or he had another job, or he was tired from traveling, or Uncle Joe came in from Burma and he hasn't seen him for twelve years. You should understand very positively that these excuses don't wash. As a general rule, you need a complete lesson plan for every day you teach. Seldom can you get by without it and do an effective job, and usually a supervisor would be justified in reprimanding you if you stumble through a lesson without a plan. This is not to say that you would be under constant supervision. In some schools, for example, a beginner may not have a supervisor observe him teach more than maybe twice a semester, or even less often. In other schools, however, a subject supervisor may observe your teaching every month and inspect your plans every week. Although regulations on supervision of teachers vary considerably, it is to your personal advantage to develop good lesson plans.

### 3. *Timing your lesson. Why it is important. How to do it.*

Your class meets for a definite amount of time, say forty minutes. You have decided on a certain topic that is to be presented during that time. How do you know it will be enough time? Or will there be considerable time left over? If so, what are you going to do? A beginning teacher, going through his material for the first time, is especially vulnerable. Of course, as you gain experience through the years, this matter of timing your lessons becomes simplified, but, even so, there are occasions when it is advisable to use a timed schedule.

You will recall that it was suggested that you carefully time your lesson on the opening day. In fact, an example of a time schedule was presented. The same process should be followed for your daily lessons until you are sure of how much material your students can absorb in a period. In particular, you may find a time schedule of advantage when your supervisor observes your teaching. On such an occasion you may be understandably nervous to some degree. Consequently, a timed lesson will help to give you a sense of security. First, you won't rush through it. Second, you won't find yourself halfway finished when the bell rings ending the period. You can eliminate minor topics if you are behind schedule, or expand important ones if you are ahead. This flexibility helps to remove tension from your teaching.

Of course it may be that a timetable for a lesson appears as a mechanical approach to your teaching. However, as pointed out in the previous paragraph, it has some definite values for the beginning teacher at the start of his career. It may prove very helpful if you write the time schedule on your lesson plan *until the sense of timing is well developed in your teaching.* Thus, for example, consider the following earth science lesson that has been given detailed timing for a beginning teacher:

PERIOD BEGINS AT 10:00, ENDS AT 10:40

*Time Schedule*
*Begin*          *End*

QUIZ

10:00          10:01          A one-minute quiz based on an important topic assigned for review and a question taken from that day's preparation. Knowing this quiz is coming every day, a student gets ready for it by reviewing his notes as soon as he enters your room— a definite aid in establishing control from the beginning of the period. Although the author used this technique with excellent results, many experienced teachers do not wish to start their lessons with a quiz. As mentioned in the previous chapter, other devices may be used. However, as a beginning teacher you may find the quiz technique very helpful to both your students and you.

*Begin*          *End*

MOTIVATION

10:01          10:05          Which of you have lived or gone to visit someone who lived by the ocean?

For those of you who haven't been near the seashore, have any of you seen a TV or motion picture showing storm waves?

How many of you have actually watched waves breaking against the shore?

What did you notice?

What other movements of the sea have
    you observed?
What shoreline features have you noticed?
Have any of you seen changes in the
    shore or beach take place from one year
    to the next?
How do you account for these changes?
Why should you care about these changes?
In what ways could they be related to
    your daily life?

(*Note:* Of course the questions used to
motivate your students would vary according to the locality they live in. Thus in
this lesson the questions would not be the
same for students living in a mountain-
ous area as if they lived close to the sea.
If done properly, these questions should
lead to the aim of the lesson. They should
convince your students why the aim of the
lesson is of value to them. Most supervisors today agree that motivation should
precede and lead in natural sequence to
a statement of the aim. Ideally the clever-
est motivation is one in which the students would be so aroused that they would
clamor for the lesson to begin. Four or
five minutes are usually allowed so that
*the motivation is sustained.* The same
kind of discussion can be aroused by reading clippings or showing pictures from
newspapers or magazines. In this lesson,
for instance, the pictures could be of
waterfront communities that suffered
shore damage after storms. Keep these
pictures in your file. Strive for excellent
motivation. It is the foundation for an
effective lesson. Unfortunately, motivating the students to want to learn is frequently the weakest part of a beginning
teacher's preparation.)

*Begin*          *End*

**AIM**

10:05          10:06          1. What is the nature of the changes in the shoreline?
                              2. What movements of the sea account for them?
                              3. In what ways could these changes possibly influence your life socially, financially, or any other way?

                              (*Note:* Elicit the aim from the students if possible. Preferably it should be stated in the form of problem-questions and written by a student on the board. Occasionally, you may have to help him in the wording.)

**MATERIALS**

                              Text, page 354–361
                              Film, #37, "Shorelines"

                              (*Note:* No time allowance is needed for materials if the film projector is to be brought in and set up by the laboratory assistant.)

*Begin*          *End*

**DEVELOPMENT**
(first part)

10:06          10:08          What is the cause of waves?

                              (*Note:* In the science department, demonstrations and visual aids are important.

|       |       | For example, a wave machine would be used here. Also, a slide or opaque projector should be included to illustrate features mentioned in this lesson.) |
|-------|-------|---|
| 10:08 | 10:09 | What controls the size of waves?<br>Ask a student to use the board to show the movements of a water particle in the sea. |
| 10:09 | 10:10 | What is the cause of currents?<br>Ask a student to explain the two types. |
| 10:10 | 10:11 | What is the cause of ground swell? |
| 10:11 | 10:12 | What is meant by the line of breakers? What causes breakers? |
| 10:12 | 10:13 | Ask students to define: surf, undertow, longshore current.<br>Ask them to use the board to show how the surf, undertow, and longshore current are formed. |
| 10:13 | 10:15 | Ask students to explain by using the board how these features are developed: sea cliff, chimney rocks. |

| *Begin* | *End* | |
|---------|-------|---|

### MEDIAL OR MIDSUMMARY

| 10:15 | 10:20 | Have the students quickly review the lesson up to this point. Clear up all doubts and misunderstandings on the first part of your development. |
|-------|-------|---|

### DEVELOPMENT
### (second part)

| 10:20 | 10:21 | Ask students to use the board to explain how these features are formed: offshore bars, spits, hooks, lagoons. |
|-------|-------|---|
| 10:21 | 10:22 | Ask students to use the board to explain |

|       |       | how these features are formed: beaches, bay-mouth bars, land-tied islands. |
|-------|-------|---|
| 10:22 | 10:34 | Show film, *Shorelines*. |

(*Note*: Regardless of the subject you teach, a beginning teacher should become thoroughly capable in the proper use of audio-visual aids.)

**SUMMARY**

| 10:34 | 10:38 | Have students summarize the important points made during the lesson and put them into their notebooks. Notes on the film should be included as part of their summary. For application, have them answer the question: Why was it worthwhile for you to study shoreline features? |
|-------|-------|---|

**QUIZ**

| 10:38 | 10:39 | A written one-minute quiz: |
|-------|-------|---|

1. How are chimney rocks formed?
2. How are lagoons formed?

(*Note:* The one-minute written quiz should be based on an important part of the lesson and summary. Use specific questions of the how or why type. Try to take questions from both parts of the lesson. If your students know that a quiz, even though it be for only one minute, is coming at the end of your lesson, they will pay sharper attention.)

**ASSIGMENT**

| 10:39 | 10:40 | Text, pages 362–370, on tides. Answer the questions on the assignment sheet. Does everyone understand the assignment? |
|-------|-------|---|

(*Note:* If you put the assignment on the board, be certain that everyone copies it.)

DISMISSAL

10:40                     Bell rings for end of period.

Experience will eliminate the need for *detailed* timing such as in the lesson above. However, you should usually be time conscious and pace your development accordingly. As a general rule, most beginning teachers find it helpful to have their first lessons carefully paced.

*4. The value of a fresh approach. Revise—discard —build anew! Present a live subject!*

You should think of new and vigorous approaches to your subject. Something different is stimulating. It may not be entirely successful at first, but it will spark your lessons. There are many interesting ways to introduce and develop any topic. Use your imagination. A fresh approach has many values. To begin with, it keeps you on your toes, doing your best to make it succeed, and this drive injects fuel for dynamic teaching. It keeps you from becoming a dull-as-dishwater teacher. Your students will appreciate the change of diet, and this makes for a better relationship with them.

To be specific, here are some suggestions:

1. Start a lesson by writing a list of ten appropriate names or terms from that day's topic. Thus, if the lesson is going to be on poetry, you could write the following: Byron, iambic, personification, "The Raven," couplet, and so forth. Call for hands of those who can explain what they mean. Go on to develop the entire lesson around these ten leads.

2. In the middle of a lesson, suddenly stop and give a quiz on what has been discussed that far as a test for alertness. A good procedure to use every week or so.

3. Give a test on that day's assignment at the beginning of the period. Have each student correct his own paper. Collect tests. Have a class discussion of assigned questions. *Give the same test again!* This time you mark the tests. Guaranteed to perk those ears the next time there's a class discussion.

4. A student becomes the teacher for that day, taking over the class under your supervision. This approach could be either given as an assignment, or as a surprise, whichever you choose.

5. Have a committee of five students from the class grade the class contributions. Have the chairman of the committee give you the averaged mark and you record it. You will be amazed at how accurately they evaluate the contributions.

6. Debates, of course, are frequently used in many subjects, especially English and history. Controversial topics give excellent material for this.

7. Reports on outside reading or individual projects, as in any of the sciences. If the assignments are made carefully, and in advance, these reports can be geared to an appropriate topic in the syllabus. This procedure develops pupil participation in the topic.

8. End the lesson on a controversial note. Some topic thrown out for discussion that is certain to arouse definite reactions for and against. Example: "Perhaps teen-agers should not be permitted to drive. Don't you think that they cause most of the accidents?"

9. You have a list of numbered questions for that day's work. You ask a student to "pick a number." That is his question. Make some questions very easy, some difficult, so that the lesson has the aspects of a game. If a weak student draws a hard question, show understanding by giving him as much credit as you can. Give him a few hints to ease his burden. He will appreciate your effort to help him. In mathematics the number could refer to the problem that has to be done at the board.

These approaches are easy for the beginning teacher to use. In fact, they are sure-fire techniques that have been developed by experienced teachers. You may do well to start with them, but spread your imagination. Constantly strive for fresh ideas. You can develop many approaches once you start to think about them. Some will be successful and others duds, but they will keep you alert to the value of a stimulating approach. In other words, don't hesitate to try something different. In this way you will build up an accomplished technique to present your subject in a provocative manner.

A further suggestion is to make notes directly on your lesson plans as you develop the various topics. *Many priceless ideas come during the progress of the lesson itself, and they most certainly should not be wasted.* Later on, you may not be able to remember them. In addition, these suggestions to yourself for improving the lesson will keep you on your toes. They help you reap the benefits of experience. The next time you present the same phase of your subject, you'll do a better job by referring to your old plans. Thus, year by year, you will become a better teacher. Some teachers throw away their lesson plans at the end of the term. This is frequently a mistake. Keep a *live* plan book, using the best of the old and adding the spice of the new! This will assist you to avoid one of the dangers of the teaching profession—falling into a rut, grinding out the same material the same old way.

It cannot be emphasized too strongly that you should constantly remind yourself to present your subject in a *vital* manner. If you get into the habit of *always* looking for a fresh approach, *always* revising, *always* building anew, your subject will stay alive even though you have been teaching it for forty years!

5. *Setting the goals. Mastering the subject. Developing the personality and character of the student. Preparing teen-agers for modern adult life.*

Actually the goals of your teaching are not as simple as they may seem at first glance. To begin with, one phase is having your students master your subject so that they can pass their examinations. Furthermore, in accomplishing the first aim, it is also your responsibility to see that your students do the very best that they can with their abilities. This puts your first goal in double focus, so to speak. The class should do well as a group (percentage of those passing at the end of the term) and as individuals reaching maximum achievement for themselves.

The second goal is the development of the teen-ager as a person. A large percentage of secondary schools now give ratings on each student's personality and character. Sometimes ten or more traits are evaluated on a superior, average, below-standard basis. These ratings may be given as many as four times a year. You realize, of course, that a weak personality or a poor character cannot be compensated for by high marks. It is your obligation to do whatever you can to improve the personality and character of the students in your classes.

Your long-range goal combines the first two and is *to bring changes for the better in the thinking, feeling, and accomplishments of your students.* You are training them in definite behavioral objectives. Consequently, activities in your classroom should bring about desired changes in personality and character. *You are preparing teen-agers for adult life.* To be successful, your students need mastery of subject skills, personality and character development, plus emotional growth. In this preparation realize that you, as a teacher, may have more influence than even their parents. It is difficult to predict how important your attitudes and training may be in the lives of your students.

But how do you implement these goals? The following suggestions will usually bring favorable results:

1. *Mastering the subject.* Excellent lesson plans supplemented by repeated review. As mentioned, one technique— there are others of course—is to try a daily quiz on a review topic. Go over the material, *each time with a new approach,* until it is firmly entrenched. It insures almost everyone passing. There are those, the very few, who fail. We shall discuss them in a later chapter.

2. *Personality and character development.* Keep your eyes and ears open. You do a student no favor when you look the other way because you will become involved. Let him know

that there are standards that he must make himself measure up to. Take the trouble to help him help himself. Explain that he must achieve personality and character development by his own efforts. Although at the moment he may resent you, he knows that underneath the reprimand you have his interest at heart.

3. *Preparation for the future.* Emphasize repeatedly that secondary school is an important step into the student's future. For one thing, he is establishing his scholarship and citizenship record. If he decides to go to college, transcripts are required. Explain that employers often send to the secondary schools for an applicant's record.

4. *Your attitude.* Develop a sturdy philosophy that your students are reaching adulthood and it is your obligation to prepare them to meet the challenge of modern life. Don't forget that emotional growth is extremely rapid during adolescence. *A sympathetic ear is sometimes the greatest need in a teen-ager's life.*

In achieving these goals, realize the need for wide horizons. Make a conscious effort not to become a curmudgeon with limited views, teaching dry-as-dust material with old-fashioned drill techniques. Your goal is to teach for a fuller life—a richer and more understanding one of which college or business may be a part. Your teaching philosophy should be that *you are responsible for more than the immediate needs of your class.* There is another world outside the four walls of your room, and your students will someday face its challenge. Reach beyond instruction of factual knowledge. Mastery of subject material is vital to school success, yet it is not the end-all purpose of life. Although control and instruction are emphasized throughout this book because of their importance to an inexperienced teacher, *there is a larger goal beyond them that you should visualize.* For example, a science teacher instructs not for mere content of subject matter, but for scientific literacy; development of avocational interests such as hobbies like mineral and rock collecting; development of scientific attitudes, appreciations (the world is very old), and, more vital than anything else, the character, hopes, and dreams of the student. In the final analysis, it is the preparation for a full, rounded life for your students that is the all-important goal of your teaching.

*A warm personality with an understanding heart for the teen-ager and his problems is essential.*

## 6. Setting the pace for the student and you.

Earlier we mentioned that you have a term plan. In some schools subject supervisors may give you a term schedule, and you may be expected to be on a certain topic by a certain date. This naturally regulates your basic pace. But in general don't be a slave to any plan. It is usually advisable to teach a few things well, rather than just covering ground—in either a plan or a text. With your supervisor's permission, revise as needed.

There are basically three groups of students—honors, average, and slow—and some modifications in both methods and content may be expected to help each one for its particular needs. Indeed, in some large secondary schools their classes are formed as "honors," "average," or "slow," and are given identifying nomenclature. (In addition, some schools have a further classification of physically handicapped.) If you are teaching in such a school, you may be working with a syllabus that has been adjusted by the subject supervisor to fit the ability of the classes you have. Thus honors classes are expected to cover a wider range of content and to probe deeper. There will be additional reading, outside reports, and special projects. The average classes will take the straight syllabus. The slow classes are composed of students unable to grasp difficult subject matter. As a consequence, the material for them will be limited in scope and depth. Considerable repetition and drill will usually be necessary. As a beginning teacher, it is up to you to adjust yourself quickly to the needs of these different groups.

But there is a pace for you, too. When you begin your teaching day, you are rested and at your best. By late afternoon, when you face your last class, the story has changed. You may have climbed four flights of stairs twice. You may have had a rough assignment controlling four hundred students in the lunch-room. Or an unfortunate incident calling for disciplinary action may have tapped your emotional reserves. Or perhaps all of these situations occurred in one day! And now you are expected to face that last class with the same pep you did the first one? Don't be silly. No one can. So what do you do?

You have to learn to pace yourself for the day. It is not a complete answer. But it is probably the best one. We are human. There is a limit to our emotional and physical endurance. We get tired. And the beginning teacher, in particular, is under additional strain because of his lack of experience.

Imagine yourself as being in a long-distance foot race. If you run with all your strength the first half mile, your chances of winning are dim. In fact, you may not even finish. Instead, you pace yourself. By repeatedly running over the course, you learn how much of your energy to expend as you go, reserving enough stamina for that last dash to the tape. Assume the same attitude for your classes. When you are teaching the first class, don't exhaust yourself. Keep reminding yourself that there is also that last class with its thirty students, and they are entitled to their portion of your drive and enthusiasm.

### 7. Use the dynamic approach in presenting your subject.

One of the mistakes made by some beginning teachers is to take the viewpoint that, because they are inexperienced, they owe their classes an apology. They present themselves to their students in a diffident manner. Such an attitude deprives them of a dynamic approach. Successful teaching demands confidence in yourself. It is possible, of course, for you to make an error and for a student to catch it. The handling of this situation we shall deal with later. Suffice to say at this point that you should go to your classes well-prepared with excellent lesson plans. Permit your students to express themselves, but *always* under your control. To achieve this, you cannot afford a diffident approach. If you do, control problems may develop.

### 8. When there's a sudden gap in your lesson, "The show must go on"—or they may lose interest.

One of the difficulties that beginning teachers sometimes get into is that suddenly the lesson stops dead. This usually happens when going to a section that has not been too well integrated with the preceding material. Of course timing your lesson, as suggested, may help to prevent these gaps. But, even so, they can occur, and the beginning teacher is at a loss as to what to do. To make matters worse, at such a time the inconsiderate students— there may be some if you have a difficult class—are likely to become disorderly. If left unchecked, such a class may become unruly. There is one remedy that is simple yet usually effective: At the first sign of a gap in the lesson, immediately pin a leading question on one of those who is prone to misconduct.

Another cause for a gap in your lesson is to begin a personal discussion with an individual on the merits of his participation in the lesson, his theories, or what have you. Immediately the rest of the class will sense your dropping of them and they often begin chattering. Actually, it is as if a signal light went on granting them permission to hold conversations with each other.

Beginning teachers tend to fall prey to either one or both of these hazards, so take care. The lesson should proceed from the moment the bell rings at the start of the period to the closing bell. *Seldom can you afford to shift your attention from the lesson and the entire class.*

Occasionally it may happen that there is a legitimate pause. For instance, the motion picture projector suddenly fails because its light bulb burned out. At such a moment it is best to say, "You people excuse me for a moment or two while I replace the bulb." Thus you maintain your control with the understanding that the presentation of your material will continue shortly.


### 9. Emphasize the important. Aim for the bull's-eye!

Obviously different sections of a lesson are of different degrees of importance. Learn to emphasize the key points. This calls for some careful forethought before you present your material. True, you have definite topics to cover within that period. But within the lesson itself some items are of more significance than others.

As a beginning teacher your aims should be:

1. A single principle or a single generalization, or a few facts well-taught.

2. Everyone knowing the lesson thoroughly.

These aims sound simple, yet achieving them is anything but that. One of the basic differences between the experienced teacher and the beginner is that the beginner scatters his efforts over a wide front rather than concentrating on the difficult parts of the lesson.


### 10. Keeping on schedule. Three suggestions.

As a teacher in the secondary school system, you should keep close to scheduled material for each day. Beginning teachers in particular tend to wander from the immediate aim of the lesson. There are times, of course, when diversions may prove helpful, especially when a member of the class, or you for that matter, may have had a personal experience that is apropos. For example, you may be discussing time belts and the international date line. One of your students may have crossed the date line or have relatives living in a different time belt. This would be a personal element worth spending a few minutes on. As such it has value and deserves a place in your presentation. However, a warning is necessary against the hazard of letting youngsters sidetrack you by getting you going on your personal anecdotes—an ancient evasive device to push the lesson aside.

Sometimes, in spite of your best efforts, you do not finish a lesson. Perhaps there is a fire drill or an assembly program that runs badly overtime. You have another full lesson coming up the next day. Three suggestions for getting back on schedule are:

1. Avoid starting where you left off the previous day. So far as possible each lesson should be a unit *with a distinct aim for the day.*

2. If it is necessary to pick up a vital point in the previous day's lesson, do it yourself. Discuss the topic *briefly,* and ask if there are any questions. Make the answers thorough, but do not elaborate. As soon as possible get to the present lesson.

3. Many experienced teachers follow the procedure of asking, "Are there any questions on yesterday's lesson?" If a hand or so shows, they answer those specific questions and then proceed directly to that day's work.

Do not make the mistake frequently made by beginners of rushing through some topics and dawdling over others. Often this is caused by your personal preferences for certain topics. For example, a physics teacher may enjoy teaching about electricity, whereas the topic of light doesn't interest him so much. Normally, present a topic on schedule.

*11. Five suggestions on classroom strategy. What should your attitude be?*

You should have a definite procedure in mind as to how you are going to conduct your lesson. Whom are you going to call upon? Will you depend on volunteers? How are you going to distribute your questions? You don't, of course, sit down and write answers to these questions, but you should have a definite approach. It should not be a matter of chance.

You may find the following suggestions helpful:

1. Strive to call on every student every day. You may seldom achieve this goal, but it should be your aim. (The old-fashioned "recitation"—where a student recited memorized answers to questions on a prepared lesson and was graded accordingly—has generally passed away. Today we prefer to use a student's answer—without the pressure of evaluating his contribution—as a device to arouse class interest through discussion. This procedure stimulates spontaneity and an atmosphere in which students are not afraid to ask questions.)

2. Use a criss-cross pattern when asking for contributions to the lesson, skipping around the room, from row to row, front to back. For example, today you might call upon your students in the following order (number one first, number twenty-five last):

| 12 | 22 | 16 | 19 | 14 |
|----|----|----|----|----|
| 5  | 9  | 3  | 2  | 7  |
| 23 | 20 | 25 | 11 | 21 |
| 17 | 15 | 8  | 24 | 18 |
| 1  | 6  | 13 | 4  | 10 |

*Order of Calling upon Students*

3. Be sure you change the order of calling upon students every day. This will help to prevent you from developing "teacher's pets." Thus, you began in the front of the first row today, start at the back of the last row tomorrow. Your students should seldom know who is going to be called upon next.

4. Most experienced teachers are opposed to grading a student every time he is called upon on the ground that it produces a stilted lesson and a restrained attitude in the students. Keep in mind that students' answers are used as springboards to start challenging discussions.

5. Avoid use of "recitation cards." These are ruled for dates and have spaces for grades. They have the disadvantage that you should remember to shuffle them, or Sam will soon know that he won't be called upon until after Mary. On the other hand, if you shuffle them every day, it may be that some students will get more opportunities to contribute to the lesson than others. Another fault is that recitation cards destroy spontaneity, a very desirable quality in dealing with teen-agers. The students are put under constant pressure. Consequently, stimulating discussions and volunteering become difficult.

A most important part of your strategy, believe it or not, is your attitude as you face your classes. Remember that fundamentally *you are in that room to help them.* In a way difficult to describe they catch your spirit.

You should keep two points firmly in mind: First, you want to remove the shadow of despair and fear of failure from the students who are not very capable. Don't be sarcastic and nasty to students because they have limited mental ability. As you know, they can't help that. Second, the brightest students are grasping for very high marks, the top of the honor roll. Give them the opportunity and the challenge that they need. These are our gifted students many of whom will go on to become our outstanding citizens.

One important fact should be made clear from your attitude: The class and the individuals in it should help themselves, even though you recognize that you are there to help them. *But you are the guide; they do the work.* If you convince them of this, and make sure they succeed, you will have wonderful classes. As the saying goes, nothing succeeds like success. This is especially true in dealing with teen-agers.

## 12. How to present your subject in a dynamic manner.

A beginning teacher should realize the importance of the manner in which he presents his subject. The following suggestions are usually helpful.

1. *Movement.*   Walk back and forth across the front of the room. Go down the aisles. On occasion stand in back of the room. Be in and around the class. Become a physical part of your students. Do not sit behind the desk, lean on your elbows, and stare out the window. No matter how significant material may be, if it is delivered lackadaisically, classes will rarely respond.

2. *Gestures.*   Point to the chalkboard. Nod your head in approval at a good point. Commend a student for an excellent response, "Bravo!" "Splendid!" "Exactly!" Such praise makes a bright spot in his day. Shake your head at someone turning to hold a personal conversation. Use your hands in expressive gestures. Swing your arms. Shrug your shoulders. Hammer your fist into your palm to drive home a point. Don't stand before your classes like a statue.

3. *Facial expressions.*   Don't hesitate to scowl when a student pulls a boner. Smile broadly at a clever answer. When something humorous is said, laugh. Oh, what wonders are accomplished by the teacher who smiles and laughs! In other words, be human. Let them know you've got feelings and that you enjoy being with them. It tightens the bond between you.

4. *Courtesy.*   Make a point of being polite to your classes and to the individuals in them. It gives a touch of dignity to your lesson. This is frequently more effective than you may believe. What you should remember is that you are building an atmosphere for your classroom. Make it one that they want to enter.

5. *Personal appearance.*   Teen-agers are especially conscious of good grooming by their teachers. Remember, you are no longer Joe College. You, as a person, are associated in their minds with your subject. If your appearance is untidy, it is that much more difficult to have them take your subject seriously.

6. *Manner of speech.*   How you talk to your classes is important. Your voice should reflect an inner, intense drive for them to get the points of the lesson. Convince them of your

sincerity and that what you are saying is important. Also, try to be certain that every student can hear you. Your voice should carry to the back of the room at all times. In addition, avoid talking down to your students or constantly using slang expressions. As a teacher, they expect you to have a command of the best English.

7. *Acting ability.* Effective teaching in secondary schools frequently calls for some dramatic ability. Ideally you should portray the part of a character dedicated to putting across his scene. Basically every subject offers some opportunity for. drama. Of course this calls for a live-wire projection of your personality upon the class.

# CHAPTER 3

# *Presenting and Evaluating Material Effectively*

*1. Finding the roots of class success.*

Inasmuch as a class is composed of individuals varying considerably in abilities and attitudes, it is reasonable to expect that one class may differ from another. Even when classes have been carefully graded for ability and accomplishment, this will nearly always still be evident. The class develops a group personality. Thus you may find that a story or joke in one class barely gets a smile, while in another class it is genuinely enjoyed. Again, you will perhaps notice that some of your classes are more unruly than others, although you can perceive no apparent cause. It is important to understand that this situation is customarily to be expected.

But whatever the characteristics of a class, it is important for you to *establish a feeling of mutual confidence*. It is your responsibility to have each class pulling with you. To help you do this, keep the following points in mind:

1. Teen-agers respect knowledge. One of the surest ways to lose your class is to try to bluff yourself through a lesson. Students have an uncanny ability to spot the teacher who is pretending knowledge he doesn't have. Occasionally you may be asked to take charge of a class temporarily, perhaps because of absence of its regular teacher. If so, you should not pretend

knowledge of that subject if you don't have it. Of course in your own subject you should be thoroughly prepared. But even so, something may arise that you don't know. Then admit your short-coming. Oddly enough, this is an excellent opportunity to draw the class closer to you! Pick two or three capable students to look up the answer and report it to the class. If they can't find it, then you give the answer which you have, of course, mean-while ascertained. They will respect your frankness and it makes you a part of the class in quest of knowledge.

2. Are you in the way of your students? This may sound strange, but not infrequently teachers block their students. For example, the class is intelligent and eager, but you dawdle over inconsequentials. Or, if the class is slow, you rush ahead while it flounders behind you. It is important to realize that in addition to the general grouping of students, previously men-tioned, into honors, average, and slow, there is a wide variation within each of these groups. For example, you may have five average classes, but each of these will have its own range of capabilities.

3. Do you believe that a class learns what you teach it? A beginning teacher is likely to think that instruction and learning go together, but this is not necessarily so. In fact, you can have a lesson plan, put your heart and soul into its delivery, and the class comes out at the end of the period shaking its head. It is generally advisable to check constantly that the class understands *as you progress through the lesson*. In the main, *do not assume that the learning process is taking place. This is extremely important.*

## 2. Do you know how to test your students to get the best results?

Each procedure you establish with your classes is for the purpose of helping them. The testing process is no exception. In addi-tion, testing should also be designed to improve your instruction.

There are many opinions as to what kind of tests to give and when to give them, but the fundamental concept remains that in secondary schools testing is primarily to improve the learning, not for marks. All of your tests, with possibly rare exceptions, should have a diagnostic purpose. Ask yourself these questions: Which students are weak? What are their *specific* shortcomings? How can I help them?

Commonly a system of grading is used, generally on a five-letter basis, although some schools have a percentage system. Both of these point out to the student his position in two respects:

1. His relative place in the class.

2. His apparent mastery of the subject.

You, however, should have some reflections to make. If practically everyone in your class has a low mark, something is wrong. *It could be with you.* Keep that in mind. If students who seem to be doing very good class work collapse on a test, what went wrong? Did you give proper evaluations? Were the questions too difficult? Was the test too long? These and similar questions should come to your attention.

Here are some important rules to follow in giving tests:

1. Study the technique for the construction of tests: the thought-provoking question versus the factual question; the question based on home study versus the question based on class discussion. Also, study sources to determine proper standards such as textbooks on testing, teacher guides, and previous examinations by experienced teachers.

2. As in other areas of teaching, don't hesitate to experiment. Try different types of tests. Find those which are most effective for your subject and your method of presentation.

3. Basically there are two types of tests, objective and essay (with shades in between). Each has its advantages. Generally use the objective to cover a large amount of content for detailed information, and the essay for comprehension of principles and procedures, and for training pupils in the organization of material.

4. Some experienced teachers make a different test for each class. *This is additional work, but many teachers believe it pays dividends.* Assume you have five classes of first-term Eng-

lish. Obviously some members of the last class to be tested could easily get word of the questions that the first class had. This is manifestly unfair and the students themselves usually appreciate your taking the trouble to insure that your tests are fair to everyone. Of course you could make one *objective-type* test with a *large number of items* (a minimum of fifty) and inform your students that *all* classes will have results tabulated in *one* distribution. Thus the first period student who gives information to a last period student automatically lowers his own relative position.

5. Balance your tests. There should be a few difficult questions to challenge the brighter students, along with some simple questions that everyone can get. The bulk of the test should be geared for the average student.

6. Tricky tests are bad medicine. They do not help the students and they mark you as insincere. Strive to make your tests absolutely reasonable and fair.

7. It is generally better to give many short tests than a few long ones. Frequently, brief tests keep your students on their toes. The weekly test is excellent.

8. Check your tests carefully before administering them. It is surprising how frequently teachers make errors or give incomplete statements that confuse students. Take the trouble to construct tests that accurately measure achievement. A poor test is worse than worthless. It is detrimental to everything you are trying to accomplish.

9. The daily quiz is frequently of tremendous value, especially to a beginning teacher. It helps you to know how thoroughly you are putting the material across. At the same time it builds up the confidence of the class in your ability to help them succeed because it gives early warning of possible failure.

10. Mark the tests and return them by next day if at all possible.

11. The same day the test is returned, go over it with the students. Take the trouble to have them understand where they made their mistakes. *Helping your students master your subject is generally considered the most important reason for giving a test.*

12. Encourage students to take notes of the questions

they missed and the correct answers. From going over their mistakes, the weaker students in particular get a sense that you are trying to help them succeed.

### 3. *The necessity for a professional attitude.*

As a general rule, remember the dignity of your position in your classroom. You are the teacher and it is generally considered improper for a teacher to mingle with the students as if he were one of them. Frequently this is a trouble spot for a beginning teacher, since he wants to be "friends" with his students, but because of lack of experience he doesn't know where to draw the line between a cordial relationship and fraternization. Young as you may be, as a teacher you are somewhat in the position of a parent and that is the way your students should, and usually do, view you.

Of course you should be interested in the school affairs of the students such as dances, plays, football, baseball, and swimming meets. Later on we shall speak of this aspect more fully. But rarely is a relationship where any student in the class can walk up and slap you on the back conducive to effective teaching. As the saying goes, familiarity breeds contempt. If you permit freedom from all formality, you may eventually be faced with impertinence. And that is something you can seldom afford.

Teen-agers in particular are in a world by themselves, and frequently attempts you make to become one of them belittles you in their eyes. Indeed, they tend to respect authority. A milk-sop generally has their contempt.

Think of other professional attitudes such as the doctor's, lawyer's, or banker's. You can expect a certain dignity and exactness of treatment. That doesn't mean they are not interested in your welfare. On the contrary, you are usually convinced that they are down-to-business and capable of helping you in your difficulty.

Until you strike the happy blend of your particular personality with your class, ordinarily lean toward developing

an extra firm professional attitude. This often gives the inexperienced teacher added self-assurance in presenting his subject.


## 4. *The importance of your enthusiasm.*

Your enthusiasm for your subject, as reflected in your daily lesson, has already been mentioned. However, enthusiasm is of such
extreme significance in achieving successful teaching that its
value should be stressed. It would be an unusual teen-ager who
would be enthusiastic about a subject if his teacher were indifferent. In fact, his common reaction would be, why should I
care if my teacher doesn't? As you know, in college work a
student generally masters the material to a large extent by himself. For the most part, he trains himself in this attitude. Many
beginning teachers carry over this college approach and expect
secondary school pupils to have that ability. Of course they frequently don't.

The teen-ager customarily needs to have his imagination fired and usually this cannot be done unless you show
enthusiasm for your subject. As a rule, the basic problem in the
motivating of any student to prepare a lesson in secondary
school is the arousal of pupil participation, and *the starting point
is frequently your own enthusiasm.* With teen-agers enthusiasm
is contagious. Youthful, they naturally resent boredom and are
constantly on the alert for something to stimulate their interest.
As their teacher, you should be sharply aware of this need. You
cannot sit behind your desk, yawn, idly tap your pencil, and
expect them to be enthusiastic about your subject.


## 5. *How assertive should you be?*

All of us have different personalities. You may be an aggressive
type of person who would tend to ride rough-shod over his classes.
As a result you would be resented. Another teacher may have

gentle mannerisms, and he is tagged as being a wishy-washy. Study yourself carefully. It is worthwhile to give this aspect of your teacher-personality considerable thought. Of the extremes mentioned, you would not want to be either one. Obviously you should be thoughtful of your students, but at the same time you should have vigorous handling of your lesson.

Certainly you should convey the impression that you are in charge of what is going on. As a general rule, don't hesitate to push the important aspects of the lesson. Seldom compromise on the issue of preparedness of the assignment. At the same time, take into account the nature of the boy or girl contributing to the lesson. Don't bellow at a demure fourteen-year-old girl because she speaks in too soft a voice for everyone in the class to hear her. Ask her to speak up so that she can be heard, but make sure your own voice reflects concern for her problem. On the other hand, you may have a loud mouth who delights in shouting whenever he can, and you should tone him down. The not-so-bright should be led gently and persistently. The bright-but-unmotivated should have their interest aroused. These developments are typical of those that require judgment and skill on your part. Your firmness in handling them will be a reflection of your personality. The one guide to have in mind is that *you should control situations so as to get the best conditions for your classes.*

### 6. Audio-visual aids. Their importance in today's teaching. Their difficulties and how to avoid them.

Audio-visual aids have become an important factor in modern instruction. It is advisable that as a beginning teacher you take advantage of them. As is to be expected, the amount and type of equipment available differs considerably from school to school. Also, the amount and type of visual-aid material that can be used effectively in your classes varies with the subject. However, audio-visual aids definitely have an important role in today's teaching technique. But there are possible problems in presentation. You should consider the following factors.

1. *Worthwhileness.* Follow the general rule of making certain that the visual-aid material is significant to what you are teaching. Thus the importance of previewing is apparent. Rarely show films, TV, or slides unless they make a contribution. They should seldom be used as a substitute for teaching because you didn't prepare a lesson plan. Remember that commonly the test is not whether the material is entertaining, but whether it advances the students' mastery of the subject and the immediate goal of the lesson. Some of the new stuff in audio-visual is truly excellent. Well selected, a documentary or top film or tape can do a special kind of teaching that no teacher can.

2. *Timing.* Whenever audio-visual aids are used, you should be careful that you have allowed sufficient time in the period. For this reason many teachers make it a rule to show illustrative material at the beginning or middle of the period. Putting it at the close of the lesson as a rule is risky because the bell may ring before you are finished and this weakens its punch. Of course you should put the audio-visual aids where they will be most effective for your particular lesson.

3. *Preparation.* Some secondary schools have a laboratory assistant who will bring in the equipment, draw the shades, and check that everything is ready. On the other hand, if you have to take care of these details, you should make all arrangements *before the lesson begins.* Last-minute preparations are largely taboo. Of course learn how to use all equipment and, needless to say, visual material should be previewed for suitability —already mentioned, but extremely important for a beginning teacher.

4. *Interruptions.* Before you start, you should realize that the unexpected may occur. Somehow, it always does just when everything seems to be going smoothly. Isn't it so? The light bulb burns out on the projector. The tension spring breaks. The film was wound backward. Or the wrong film was delivered. When you plug in, you get no current. Halfway through, the film breaks. Or, if you're showing a sound film, the fuse blows for the speaker. All you get is silence. What do you do? Grin, crack a joke. If you

can't make your repair quickly, then forget about the visual-aid for that day. *Don't fuss and fume.* Remember that you should get through the assigned material. Be prepared to present the material by other means.

5. *Temptation for disorder.* In some schools where strong behavioral control is needed, this factor is not to be minimized. In fact, in classes where misconduct is a problem, it is the reason why some teachers are reluctant to use audio-visual aids. In the darkened room it is easy for mischief-makers to play their games. Kicking, pinching, pulling hair, shooting clips, zooming paper airplanes, giggling, and croaking are some of the commoner activities that may be found with unruly teen-agers. However, audio-visual materials are definitely an important part of instruction in many subjects, and *you* run the class. *Be alert.* If you are beginning your teaching career in a difficult school, at the first sign of disorder, stop the presentation and snap on the lights. Admittedly, in a darkened room it is sometimes difficult for you to be sure of the mischief-maker, so you will have to be wary that you don't make a mistake. It would be better to ignore than to falsely accuse—don't blame someone without positive evidence. But you should turn on the lights and quit showing the audio-visual material until the class is quiet and in order. Of course if you are sure who the mischief-maker is, have him stand beside you. Put out the lights and proceed. Repeat this process if necessary. Of course give a reprimand and suitable punishment to those who disrupted your presentation. With the average class, however, you will usually not find disorder a problem. Of course in a superior school seldom would you have any concern about behavior.

6. *Check.* You might try the technique of stopping the presentation for questions, or sometimes shutting off the sound to minimize the development of a passive attitude. Furthermore, in order that your classes pay careful attention to the visual material, *some type of summation is usually advisable.* This could be:

a. Brief oral quiz.
b. Written summary.
c. Comparative evaluations by the students.

### 7. Is the daily written quiz advisable?

The technique of a daily written quiz has been mentioned repeatedly. Because its advisability is frequently questioned, we shall now consider it more thoroughly. As already brought out, most teachers do not like to give a written quiz every day. They claim it is monotonous and makes for a stilted lesson. They doubt its effectiveness, feeling that a quiz motivates students after a fashion, but daily it could become routine and less meaningful. Furthermore, they point out, a considerable amount of correction work is involved, and this is under pressure because papers should be marked and returned by the following day. In addition, grades should be entered. This work, coupled with the making of lesson plans, becomes a heavy nightly burden.

On the other hand, the daily written quiz is widely recognized by many experienced teachers as a valuable procedure. They point out that a great deal depends upon the manner in which it is given as to whether it is monotonous, dull, and ineffective. It can be a stimulating challenge that helps to keep all classes prepared at all times and gives each student a sense of daily accomplishment. By its faithful use few students get "lost." As for the paper work involved, various compromises are frequently used, for example:

1. Limit the quiz to *two* questions, one on an assigned *review* topic, and one on that day's *advance* assignment. (Many teachers prefer this procedure.)

2. Ask only *one* question—either review or advance.

3. Each class is warned to be ready for a quiz. It is given to *one* of the classes, skipping around to various classes on different days, so that the classes never know which one will get the written quiz that day. (Some teachers like this method because it injects something of the game element—who's next?)

The strongest advocates claim it may be decidedly worthwhile to tax *all* your classes with a quiz *every* day, *without fail*, because frequently it does wonders for control and mastery of content. Some of these teachers consider the written daily quiz so important that they give it at the beginning of the lesson. Others prefer to reserve it for the end of the lesson and then include it as part of the summary. They believe that it would be especially worthwhile as a technique for beginning teachers to use.

And so we have conflicting viewpoints as to whether the daily quiz is advisable. Perhaps, as possibly in other educational procedures, the answer lies in your own class's responses and your preferences in how to effectively help your students.

If you decide to try the daily written-quiz technique, some suggestions about marking the papers might be helpful. Let's discuss them next.

### 8. Do students mark papers? Is only the teacher permitted to evaluate?

In some schools there is a prohibition by the administration against having students correct papers. For teachers in these schools the matter is closed. But as a rule you are permitted to have students mark quizzes used primarily for instruction. In general, only teachers should mark major tests. For example, midterms or finals should be graded by you. Sometimes, however, permission is granted to have competent students mark the objective-type questions in these examinations.

If regulations permit, select students as your assistants. Usually two or three will be sufficient. Commonly such students are referred to as secretaries and their duties, in addition to grading quiz papers, will be to check homework papers, laboratory exercises, book reports, and such.

Another suggestion is that you use a rotation system, which calls for selecting two *different* students each day from each class. If there are thirty-five students in a class, everyone gets a chance each month to mark the quiz papers.

The rotation system has these advantages:

1. There is practically no burden on anyone to grade the daily quiz papers. Less than once a month would a student have to mark them.

2. Everyone shares in the marking so that there are no "teacher's pets."

3. A spirit of cooperative enterprise is engendered. The class feels that everyone is working to help everyone else.

4. It emphasizes to the student the importance of helping himself. It does away with any pupil-versus-teacher attitude. The teacher is not marking the failures—the class is. This puts you in a strong position.

5. It sharpens the competitive spirit, a most desirable asset usually. When a not-so-bright has his opportunity to mark the quiz, he is definitely on the prowl to catch one of the "brains" of the class. And it does happen!

When the quiz papers are returned the following day, the failures should be put on top so that you can immediately question those students as to "how come?"

What are the disadvantages of the rotation system? The main objection raised is that dishonest students will cheat on marking their papers, or that favoritism will be shown to their buddies. Such things do happen, of course, but it is amazing how infrequently such occasions arise. Besides, you would be on your guard and use discrete checking on your own. You will usually find that perhaps the first week or so there may be an incident or two, but once the class catches the spirit that it is helping itself, improper marking is generally negligible.

Other types of student-marking tests such as exchanging papers and having the marker sign his name can be used. The customary cautions apply. This device has the advantage of promptness wherein students are immediately informed of their errors.

Finally, some schools do have scoring machines.


## 9. How frequently should you review?

The necessity for review generally varies with the subject and the ability of the class. Sometimes material contains much of its own review as you advance. For example, the fundamental processes of algebra are repeated as progress is made. In language, yesterday's vocabulary is used in all lessons that follow. But in history you frequently find material that stands by itself. For example, what were the causes for the Revolutionary War? They are not the same as for the Korean conflict. Thus we tend to have a greater need for review. In science there are many isolated topics that can be forgotten or confused in the student's mind, and review frequently becomes a necessity. For example, the principles of weather forecasting have little to do with the study of astronomy. We see then that aside from a variation in the need to review according to subject, there may also be considerable difference in topics within a subject. Obviously topics that are confusing or difficult should be reviewed frequently.

Also the factor of ability to grasp and retain regulates the amount of review. To illustrate, a moderate-sized secondary school will have sixteen or more classes of freshman English. When graded, these vary all the way from exceptionally bright to extremely limited. Thus the need for review may differ considerably from class to class.

It is understandable, accordingly, that the amount of review required for a particular class and subject is left very largely in your hands. There is a tendency for all of us to think that once we have taught something, the class understands and retains it. Consequently, there is a constant urge to push forward. Who want to go over old stuff? And of course there is the crowded syllabus. Somehow it is always packed with more material than we can possibly cover and do a thorough job. The result is that review, considered by many teachers so vital to successful learning, is frequently shoved to the rear unless we make a careful niche for it.

Consider these suggestions:

1. Have a definite schedule for review of important topics that your students *must* master.

2. Have an assignment sheet for review topics. Thus with the advance assignment, there is usually a review one.

3. At the *very beginning* of the period *every day* allow students a few minutes to study their review notes. This emphasizes the importance of review to them.

4. Give a one-question written quiz picked at random

from the review topics for that day. You will note that this fits in with the daily written quiz schedule already discussed.

The immediate result of this steady diet of review is that it usually gives your students immense confidence. And isn't this important? Furthermore, a planned review of this type keeps your finger on the pulse of your class. A diagnosis of the strong points and weaknesses of your students is frequently helpful to them and useful to you. As a rule, constant, careful review lets you know exactly how well prepared they are for their examinations. You want as many students to pass as possible with the highest grades they can get. And regular, thorough review is nearly always needed for this success. Remember, though, in spite of the goal of subject success, that *your teaching should* **NOT** *emphasize marks.* Marks are important, but don't let the means used to obtain them defeat your ends. It might be said that a student's grades are his pay for his work. And you want your students to learn your subject. But these reasons are only part of why you are teaching. You are striving to reach the worthier accomplishment of your students' preparation to face adult life.

## 10. The art of asking questions.

Keep in mind that the primary purpose of asking questions is to help the student. Therefore, questions should be carefully phrased so that they are understood. Sometimes a question reveals that the student has not prepared his work. Other times it shows that you have not made the matter clear. Indeed, questions are one of the basic tools with which you pry out the weaknesses of pupil *and teacher*. It is generally recognized that effective questioning is at the very heart of superior teaching. Commonly it is the key for unlocking the interest of your class and developing your entire lesson. A good question ignites the thinking process and demands that a student apply his knowledge.

Of course your questions should be an integral part of the lesson, serving as a challenge to stimulate the thinking you wish to arouse, or as prongs to reach for needed factual material. Therefore *considerable thought should be given to the questions you are going to ask,* and usually they should be written into your lesson plan.

As your lesson unfolds, be careful to ask *thought-provoking, pivotal questions in sequential order.* Thought-provoking questions furnish new ideas and enable you to expand the development of your lesson. The following is an example of a thought-question: Why did the first colony at Roanoke disappear?

As a beginning teacher, cultivate the art of asking stimulating questions in their best form. *Learn to be careful how you state your question.* Here are some suggestions to keep in mind:

1. Rarely put the question in the form that will call for a simple *yes* or *no* answer, such as "Did Edgar Allan Poe write *The Raven?*"

2. Avoid the guessing question, such as "Is *The Deserted Village* a poem or a novel?"

3. Short questions are better than long ones. Being less involved, they are easier to comprehend. The rule is, generally two short questions do a better job than one long one.

4. In most instances avoid involved questions that have subdivisions. In particular, questions where the second part is dependent upon understanding and having the correct answer to the first part. Thus the compound question such as, "How is a volcano formed and why does it erupt?" should usually be avoided. Don't forget, nearly always the purpose of questioning is to develop your lesson so that students will understand the work being done.

5. Avoid generalities and vagueness. Make your question call for specific information. Do not ask ambiguous questions such as "What happens when a man gets sick?"

6. Rarely give the answer. All the student has to do is to echo what you told him. For example, "Socrates was an Athenian philosopher. What was Socrates?"

7. Seldom furnish part of the answer, for example, "Francis Scott Key composed the words for *The Star-Spangled B ——*" Even worse, don't look for placid agreement with questions like "We drink water, don't we?"

8. Take the trouble to make certain that your question

is perfectly clear to the student. Sometimes a student fails because he doesn't understand a poorly worded question, such as "Gaseous masses are luminous bodies but not always individual stars but planets are composed of solid material but are always individual bodies but are confused with them. Why is this so?"

It is important that you get into the habit of expressing your questions properly. Note the following three examples of poor questions and observe how easily they can be improved:

1. *Poor:*

> "Charles Brown, will you please tell the class all about Napoleon?"
>
> (*Note:* First, the teacher has chosen the student who is to answer before giving the question. Therefore, many students may not listen very carefully. Second, the question is not specific. Avoid such terms as "all about.")

*Better:*

> "What in your opinion was the most important result of the battle of Waterloo? Charles Brown."
>
> (*Note:* When the question is expressed in this form, the teacher has the opportunity to use it as a stimulant to develop a class discussion, for example, "Does anyone agree with Charles?" "Why?" "Disagree?" "Why?" "What is your evidence?")

2. *Poor:*

> "The battle of Waterloo was lost by the French. Is that correct? Charles Brown."
> "Yes."
>
> (*Note:* The teacher has permitted a yes-or-no answer which gives the student a 50 percent chance of giving the correct answer without having done any studying at all. Furthermore, it deprives the student of the opportunity to express himself fully.)

*Better:*

> "Why in your opinion did the French lose the battle of Waterloo? Charles Brown."

(*Note:* As in the answer to the first question, the answer here can be used to develop a class discussion by using the same technique.)

3. *Poor:*

"Where is Waterloo located and who were the allies who fought against Napoleon? Charles Brown."

(*Note:* The teacher has asked a compound question, which is sometimes confusing to a student, especially if he has limited ability. Also, the teacher has asked two successive questions of the same student. It is advisable to skip around the class.)

*Better:*

"Where is Waterloo located? Charles Brown."

(*Note:* After the correct answer is received, the teacher proceeds to the next question and calls on a different student in another section of the class.)

"Who were the allies who fought against Napoleon? Catherine Jones."

As noted in the better phrasing of the first two questions, strive to generate stimulating discussion among the youngsters. Get your students to express *their* ideas and evaluations. This procedure tends to keep the lesson alive—perhaps argumentative but vital—and *within the class.* The old-fashioned recitation, where the pupil spouted memorized factual material to the teacher, offers little in the way of challenge to youngsters in the development of *their* thinking.

Keep your class alert with plenty of good questions. Here are some suggestions to help you improve your technique for presentation of your questions to your class:

1. Usually give a slight pause after asking a question in order to give each student the opportunity to mentally formulate his own answer. Then you call on an individual. This procedure tends to force all students to listen to the question and think about it.

2. Normally do not go around the entire class striving for an answer. This wastes valuable time. After perhaps two or

three unsuccessful attempts to get a favorable response, rephrase your question. If that fails, use a different approach. Frequently it is then best to bluntly state what you had in mind.

3. Rarely try to trick a student or confuse him. You gain nothing and you lose the warmth of your class's support. Such a procedure belies the basic principle of helping the student. It will usually breed mistrust and hostility. A cordial, yet respectful, attitude is essential to an effective teacher-pupil relationship.

4. As a general rule, give the weaker students the first opportunity to contribute to the lesson, even though the question may be a difficult one. This pulls them into the discussion. For especially weak or shy students, ask them a question that they can obviously answer. This technique for the most part saves them embarrassment and gives them a sense of belonging. Remember good teaching requires more than the presentation and mastery of facts.

5. Use the better students for confirmation. Thus to the bright boy, "What improvement would you make on that answer?" Challenge their replies for complete accuracy. Keep them on their toes. Demand the very best in scholarship to expand their potential. They are the leaders of our tomorrow.

6. Distribute questions at random, but *strive to have every student take part in the lesson.* Your aim: Each pupil makes at least one contribution every day. You won't reach them all, but try! Develop a feeling of class unity: all for one, one for all! Remember, you are not trying to catch your students, but to help them.

7. Generally speaking, don't make a habit of repeating the question. Train your students to listen carefully. Otherwise you may find yourself frequently giving the question two or three times. The exception here would be if there is a loud noise, such as pneumatic drills working on the sidewalk outside your windows, or if you know a student has poor hearing, or on occasion if a student just didn't happen to catch what you said.

8. Do not make a practice of repeating answers. There are exceptions, of course, when you wish to give emphasis on a special point in the lesson. Or, if a student wants an answer repeated, ask another student to do so.

9. Strive to keep a sharp eye on the inattentive student. Because of its importance, we repeat this suggestion in this topic. Don't hesitate to call several times on the person who is not participating in the lesson. Avoid giving the impression that once a student has made a contribution to the lesson, he won't be requested to take part again that day. Thus, rarely rely solely upon volunteers.

10. When a student makes an excellent answer to a thought-provoking question, make a point of showing that you appreciate his contribution. Congratulate him. In the main remember that the responses to your questions build the platform upon which you develop your lesson. In this connection customarily encourage your class to comment on answers and to make worthwhile additions.

11. If a student gives an answer that is the equivalent of the one you were looking for, accept it. As a rule don't expect exact word-for-word answers. Beginning teachers sometimes do this and it may be demoralizing to a class.

12. Don't forget that generally speaking the purpose of your questions is to stimulate the learning process. Therefore, encourage your students to ask questions of you and of each other. Almost always your aim is to get a live-wire presentation of that day's problem and its solution.

13. Rarely permit the class to answer a question in chorus. Normally hold the individual student responsible.

14. Of course questions should commonly be oriented toward fulfilling the aim. This emphasizes the need for usually making thought-questions an essential part of your lesson.

15. Have a friendly attitude in your questioning. Remember, you are working *with* the student, not against him. Thus, *be sure you listen carefully and patiently to his answers*. Give him the opportunity to do the best that he can.

Skillful teaching ordinarily demands an integration of stimulating questions and factual presentation. By the end of the period *every* student should have received a *definite* benefit from his participation in the lesson. In most instances to arrive at this goal, thought-provoking questions should be used from the opening motivation to the closing summary. Putting it simply, follow the general rule: *don't tell, ask.* Involve the student as much as possible by adroit questioning. It is a fine art. Develop it as soon as you can to the best of your ability.

## 11. Should written homework be assigned?

The politician's answer would be a good one for this question. "Yes and no, it all depends." Most experience has shown that there is little profit in asking students to write the homework if it is a mechanical, unchecked process. Some students can get an A+ on every lesson and test and never write a line. Others can fill pages of written homework every night and fail in all their lessons and tests.

It doesn't take long for even a beginning teacher to know that it is possible for a student to write reams of stuff and not know a thing about its essential ingredients. And then, too, some students copy written homework, getting slight, if any, benefit from it. Of course there are occasions when written homework is a must. For example, problem solving in science and mathematics, or theme writing in English.

Sometimes you run into the problem of a student who protests he has no place, time, or energy for homework. Such claims should be carefully investigated before you accept them. Sometimes there are legitimate cases where students because of economic conditions in their home must work long hours after school. But don't be gullible—check into the situation for the youngster's own good.

Whenever you assign homework make every effort to convince your students why they should do it, even though it may not be written. Base your appeal upon *their* needs. Keep firmly in mind that *the motivation for their doing the assignment should stress the vital element of how it is going to help them.* If you fail to arouse their interest, your assignment may be worse than useless. Youngsters, as well as adults, want a *reason* for doing something. In this case, that reason should not be founded upon doing homework merely because the teacher said to do it. In most instances, the purpose should go much deeper if it is to prove of lasting value. Who wants to learn something that is apparently useless? Thus, your students should be thoroughly motivated to arouse maximum interest in the assignment for the next day's lesson. It may well be that it is better to give no assignment at all if you can't motivate your students to want to do it. If your students are not interested in doing their assignment, it may amount to busywork done at home. Frequently failure to motivate students to do their homework is one of the weakest points in a beginning teacher's approach. All too often he does not take the effort to motivate properly. Youngsters need to understand *why* they should sacrifice their time—which may amount to an hour or more—in preparing for a lesson. In summary, you should be thoroughly convinced that *the assignment is worthwhile* and you should then take the trouble to show your students *how it will benefit them.*

The problem involved with written homework is that it should be checked. Consider the burden this imposes every day on a teacher. If there are thirty-five students to a class and you have five classes, that means 175 papers should be read. If we allow three minutes for each paper (a conservative estimate), you will have to take eight hours and forty-five minutes to evaluate them! But you can't sit down and just read straight through for almost nine hours. You'll need some breaks. Suppose you take a ten-minute rest every hour. That means your total time would be at least *ten hours! And this is every night of the week!* Of course that is ridiculous because you do have to eat, sleep, and wash your face. Granted that sometimes teachers have perhaps only a hundred students, or maybe even less, that still leaves a heavy nightly load of papers to mark. One of the following compromises is usually made:

1. The students keep the written homework in their notebooks. They are repeatedly told that the writing will help them concentrate and will give them notes to study. On occasion the teacher walks around the room and verifies that everyone has the homework done. Notebooks, of course, should be rated each marking period and included as part of the report card mark.

2. The written homework is collected each day and the teacher's secretary (student helper) checks that everyone has done it. In addition, the secretary can also check for completeness and legibility. Unsatisfactory papers are handed to the teacher for appropriate action. If the work is acceptable, the secretary enters a dot in the record book under that day's date. For example:

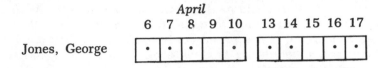

*April*

| | 6 | 7 | 8 | 9 | 10 | | 13 | 14 | 15 | 16 | 17 |

Jones, George

This system shows the teacher at the end of the marking period that the student has not settled his homework account for April 9 and 15. When made-up work is submitted, a dot is entered in the proper date space. Of course the papers should be returned to the students the next day.

3. A spot-check is made by having a class turn in its written homework without advance notice that it will be collected. This is carefully marked and returned *promptly*. Select a different class each day. Some teachers feel that the spot-check method has an element of trickery and that they wouldn't like to treat their students that way. However, many teachers believe that a class should be prepared at all times and they know that spot-checks are made so there is no deception involved.

4. Very seldom is written homework requested. When it is, then it is collected, marked, and handed back as soon as possible.

*12. The importance of keeping your mouth closed. Minimize the lecture method of teaching. Let the class express itself. Strive for discussion rather than recitation.*

One of the best ways to present your material to your classes is to get them to do most of the talking. As a general rule, the more opportunity you give your students to express themselves, the more effective your teaching becomes. *Execessive talking is often a weakness of the inexperienced secondary school teacher.*

When you do all the talking (the lecture method), the class sits back, folds its mental hands, and just listens. And after a while, as often noted, they just sit. You are talking away at a great rate, imagining that their quietness is a sign that absorption is taking place. It could be that many or even most are not learning what you are trying to teach. But, concomitantly, they may well be learning that your subject is dull and that you are a bore. They have other things to think about, you know. Dates! Cars! Games! Remember?

The lecture method of presentation has certain places where it is useful. For example, in a laboratory demonstration in physics or chemistry it is sometimes necessary. But, even here, the expert teachers try to draw as much of the needed explanations as they can from the students.

It is amazing how much babbling is usually done by an inexperienced teacher. This almost invariably has the direct result of depriving members of the class from volunteering and expressing themselves. In effect, the subject is taken away from them. The teacher is showing how much *he* knows. Always strive to keep the lesson *in* the class. Usually your comments should be few and far between, to use the common expression.

Until you learn the technique of having the students work on their lesson, a suggestion is that you write *keep your mouth closed* on slips of paper and clip them to the seating plan for each class as a reminder to yourself. *Pretend that you can't talk.* You will be surprised how the lesson will revolve around the class. By way of illustration, generally recommended times for you to speak up would be:

1. To clarify a point.
2. To give additional information which you feel is important but is not brought out in the text.

It is ordinarily better to strive for discussions rather than recitations in your classes. A discussion generally involves the whole class in the topic being presented and usually affords the opportunity for many students to become involved in the learning situation by their contributions. A recitation, however, frequently limits the viewpoint to what a particular student happens to know about a certain item. Sometimes, indeed, a recitation is merely a checkup on whether the student has memorized assigned material. Thus it can be seen that the recitation tends to isolate a student from the rest of the class, whereas a discussion as a rule functions to involve the entire class.

# CHAPTER 4

## *Building Class Attitudes*

### 1. The class as a group.

Classes are made of individuals—each with his own personality—
that possibly blend or interact with one another to give certain
characteristics to each class. Perhaps one of the most effective
aids you can have in building proper attitudes is to get an accurate evaluation of a class's positive and negative qualities. It
might be advisable to start from the first day of the term. As a
general rule each class varies in ability and attitude, resulting in
an aggregate personality. To illustrate, consider the customary
differences in ability and attitude between the junior high school
pupil and the senior high school student. In addition, there frequently is considerable variation between classes on the same
grade level. Keeping this in mind, try to analyze each of your
classes *as a group*. Make your appraisal in simple terms, crystalliz-
ing both good and bad traits, for example:

| Period of Class | Attitude of Class | Characteristics of Class |
|---|---|---|
| First | Positive | Bright, but |
| | Negative | nonlearning attitude |
| Second | Positive | Willing to work, but |
| | Negative | little ability |
| Third | Positive | Good control, but |
| | Negative | weak in participation |

| Fourth | Positive | Very bright, but |
|--------|----------|------------------|
|        | Negative | likely to become boisterous |
| Fifth  | Positive | Capable, but |
|        | Negative | poor work habits |

Sometimes an analysis of this type may help to put your finger on the strong and weak points of each class. Usually the relationship between any one of your classes and you is a delicate fabric that you should weave with extreme care. In many instances attitudes, expressed and implied, make all the difference between establishing rapport, or being mutually destructive. Frequently a "bad" class can become a "good" class when its characteristics are understood and it is properly handled. Even with limited teaching experience, you may at times observe that the same class reported by one teacher as being "difficult" is reported by another as "no problem whatsoever." It would seem that an accurate measurement of characteristics would be helpful. Sometimes it is the keystone in building acceptable attitudes.

## 2. *The segments within a class.*

Just as one class frequently varies from another in its characteristics, there are often different qualities within a single class. Even honor, average, and slow classes sometimes have distinct layers within them. It may be useful in developing the potential of your students for you to be conscious of the possible stratified nature of each class. Of course when the secondary school is large enough to provide honor and slow programming for classes, variations in ability can be a simpler problem than if there is no such division.

Although sometimes classes may be fairly homogeneous chronologically, they frequently are not. This can be true even in large schools, especially in minor subject areas. For example, there may be only four classes in earth science, even though your school has a registration of over two thousand students. Into these four classes might come freshmen, sophomores, juniors, and seniors. In addition, these students could possibly range in intellect from superior down to those of limited ability. Thus, within a single class there could be considerable variations in abilities and attitudes. The problem of development in such a class may depend to some extent upon your ability to recognize each segment. Naturally, the wider the span, the more teaching skill may be required on your part. Admittedly, this is usually a challenge that cannot be solved by attempting to treat all segments the same. However, your recognition of the problem may frequently put you one step forward. Preserve a sense of class unity, but at the same time strive to *give careful consideration to an individual's accomplishments* **IN TERMS OF HIS ABILITY**. If the segmentation is *extreme,* here are two suggestions which may help your students:

1. Give differentiated assignments.
2. Use instructional materials on different levels.

Expecting the same performance from widely different abilities and attitudes in a class is sometimes one of the earmarks of the inexperienced teacher. Generally speaking, keep in mind that *all* of your students should receive your best efforts, not only in mastery of your subject, but, more important, in attaining a sense of worthwhileness.

### 3. The "bad" days of a class. Their causes. How to meet the situation.

In spite of the fact that you might have a smoothly functioning class, there are occasional days that are partially or even totally unsuccessful. You have an excellent lesson plan and are eager for your class to appear. But when it does, nothing goes right. The class is jittery, difficult to control, and obviously uninterested. You should make a reservation in the back of your mind that this difficulty runs in the normal course of a school year and is commonly to be expected. Possible causes are:

1. Important examinations are being held. Even though these tests are not given by you, you may feel the impact. For

example, college entrance boards, midterms, finals, aptitudes, state scholarships, and so forth.

2. Just before and after a holiday are frequently difficult days.

3. Special assemblies can cause considerable excitement throughout the school. An oratorical contest. A rousing debate on a significant topic. A stimulating play.

4. A fight took place. Perhaps between two admirers of the same young lady. Or a heated argument between a teacher who lost his head and a student. Or a nasty scene between two girls. Intense emotionalism will usually upset a class.

5. Sometimes not understanding an important topic can disturb a class. For example, the balancing of equations in chemistry.

6. Weather can prove an extremely disrupting factor. An excessively hot, humid day. A raw, cold rainy day when many students get soaked before arriving in school. Or, if in a state that has snow storms, a paralyzing blizzard.

7. Important student activities may reach into your room. The prom. That all-important football game. The election of class officers. Distribution of the senior year book (everyone must sign everyone else's copy immediately or the day is lost).

8. The new texts haven't arrived. Or the books, so that they can be checked and stored, have to be collected immediately after the final exams. This leaves two or three days with a hole in the middle.

9. The day after a substitute had your class. You've been away because of illness and when you return you are alarmed by what has happened to your class. (No matter how good the substitute, he's not you!)

In other words, generally watch out for *any occasion that has unusual conditions involved.* It is normal for teen-agers to have dynamic reactions. Consequently, you should be prepared for these days because they are almost certain to come. In most instances you can best meet the situation by having a firm attitude. Although you understand the situation, strive to keep your class functioning smoothly. Sometimes an effective way to deal with this problem is as follows: Give the class a written lesson for the first fifteen minutes based on your plan for that day. This tends to calm them. Then quietly proceed with a discussion derived from the answers they wrote to your questions. Shortly before the end of the period, go to a summary of their material.

### 4. The runaway class. The signs of it. What to do.

Often the earmark of a runaway class is that control for the most part has slipped from you. It seems that no longer does the class look to you as its leader. At first the indications may not be apparent. Then gradually you find yourself being rejected by the class. For example, the students may refuse to do the assignment. Or you may find yourself threatening them with, "You'll be sorry if you don't do this." They want to see you make them feel sorry. Or you cajole. Or even beg. "Now, *please* behave. You know you can't act like this. It just isn't right. What would your fathers and mothers say?" This will probably be greeted by hoots and a gale of laughter. Sometimes the runaway class goes to the extreme of open rebellion. The students talk freely. Even get up and walk to a window.

What to do? The following procedure may prove effective:

1. Decide which students led the runaway.

2. Look up the permanent records of these leaders.

3. If there are guidance counselors in your school, go to them for additional information on the troublemakers.

4. Arrange for immediate help from your subject supervisor or the supervisor in charge of discipline. Make certain they will support you in the action you wish to take, or find out what they want to do.

5. Take the action agreed upon. Do not permit the leaders of the runaways to talk you out of your decision. They will probably offer all sorts of alibis and promises. Generally speaking, don't weaken. Make them take their medicine unless you are convinced that it is not necessary. In some instances, this is possible.

6. Watch carefully for any further outbreaks of disorder. If any occur, repeat the same dose. Remember, the runaway class should be halted, or it may cost you your job.

7. Evaluate yourself. Sometimes the difficulty, at least in part, may lie with the teacher—especially if a beginner.

## 5. *Fighting tension in a class. Three suggestions.*

Sometimes an important factor in a class is tension. Observe carefully. Is the class keyed-up? Nervous? Your personality may be such that instead of inspiring confidence, you generate fear of failure. Recall your own days as a college student and your apprehension when the professor gave an examination. Teen-agers in general frequently lack a sense of security. The marginal student in your class is often deeply conscious that it is a matter of touch-and-go, especially if you are teaching one of the more difficult subjects such as advanced mathematics or physics. On the other hand, the honor student is sweating to maintain a high average. Perhaps he is striving for a scholarship award that determines whether he goes to college or not. And there you are with your red-ink pen in hand to decide his fate. So it is very easy for tension to mount in a class. This is one of the reasons why many expert teachers consider it unwise to grade students during a lesson.

Some suggestions are:

1. Demonstrate that you are definitely sympathetic with *all* your students in their efforts to succeed. The statement, "It's almost impossible to fail in my class," is very reassuring. *But mean it.* To repeat previous advice: *Work diligently to make certain that each student is doing his best and give him the highest mark that you can.*

2. Make sure that you know your subject. A class can detect a bluffer ten times out of ten. This fact, although already mentioned, cannot be overemphasized.

3. Generate an air of buoyant self-confidence. Demonstrate that you are with your students all the way—that their

classroom problems are yours. Let them know that *you have faith in them* and they will follow your leadership.

Getting rid of class tension nearly always helps to achieve successful teaching.


## 6. The "fluid material" and intangibles of a class.

Usually a person changes more rapidly during his adolescence than at any other age. Secondary school teachers are aware of this perhaps more than anyone else. Even parents, although they can observe the swift changes in their teen-agers, are not confronted with the complexities of more than a hundred students changing their attitudes and personalities from day to day. In your classroom little demure Mabel decides she's the vamp type and next day she appears with frizzed hair, shortened dress, and tight sweater. Charley makes up his mind he's going to be a corporation lawyer and puts on a suit of manners he imagines appropriate for the legal profession. Last week John's father and mother were killed in an automobile accident, and now his world is so very different. Today Helen feels ashamed and isolated because her sister was arrested last night as a prostitute. Andrew's elated. His dad just bought a brand new thirty-foot cabin cruiser. Ethel is in love with Sam, but neither family approves. And so, on and on.

Thus you stand before fluid material constantly changing its emotional characteristics. Your profession is *the most important in the world.* Your hand is on the heart of teen-age life. There is no substitute for you. To the adolescent, your stern word or sympathetic hand at the right time can frequently make the difference between success or failure, happiness or misery.

Of course subject matter is important, but your real significance goes much deeper. You are engulfed in fluid material that is constantly changing its youthful viewpoint. Your personality reaches out to help your students resolve the uncertainties of life, such as the painful awakening to economic insecurity, a crushed dream, or the rapture of first love. Helping them to deal with these intangibles gives deeper significance to your teaching.


### 7. *How to establish a partnership with your class.*
### *Seven suggestions.*

From the moment you first meet your classes, you should be working toward establishing a close relationship. Some methods of achieving this goal are:

1. Humor is a strong lever. Use it. Tell jokes or appropriate anecdotes. *But don't overdo it.* One joke or so is sufficient in a period. Post cartoons on your bulletin board. Laugh with the class when something humorous turns up. Also, even more important, be able to laugh when the joke's on you.

2. Avoid the ugliness of sarcasm. When you are caustic you employ your superior training and knowledge to belittle rather than help. Instinctively a class will unify in rebellion. Adolescents don't mind being wrong. They are used to that. What alienates them is a nasty-tongued teacher who, they believe, despises them for their mistakes.

3. Along a similar line, be sympathetic in your corrections both in tone and mannerism. *This is extremely important to the teen-ager.* An overbearing attitude is pure vitriol.

4. Approach all lessons *with the class.* Show that you are with them each step, *as if teaching yourself.* This is a neat trick, and if you try hard enough, long enough, you can do it.

5. Be patient. You are years beyond them in learning skills. They are beginning to grasp the lower rungs of scholarship. It is your job to give them a boost, not step on their hands.

6. Use a morale-building slogan. For example, "We are working together." Say this repeatedly, in all classes every day. It has a marvelous effect. (Isn't it wonderful to know the principal is on *your* side? Well, your students want you on *their* team.)

7. Rarely berate the class as a class. If you do, they may solidify themselves against you. It's a natural reaction—a group-protective insurance policy.

*8. Evaluations by the class. Use of the daily "question box."*

At the end of the term it may be advisable to ask your classes to write a summary of the values your subject has for them and to make helpful suggestions. Your present students may be able to help you plan better lessons for next year's classes. You can frequently profit from a *pattern* that sometimes appears in student evaluations. Extreme suggestions, of course, will seldom have value.

You should realize that some students are not competent to evaluate, their comments being reflections of immature judgment. Sometimes students make impossible suggestions such as to omit whole sections of material required by the syllabus. However, although a few possibly write sheer nonsense, you may receive many worthwhile contributions.

Most teachers feel that leaving off names makes for freer expressions of opinion. That may be true, but you may then get more ridiculous comments and frequently an insincere approach. Try both methods and see which is more successful for you.

The "question box" is frequently a worthwhile teaching aid. For most effectiveness the students' questions should be based on topics under discussion.

*9. Class image. Two suggestions for improving it.*

Each class tends to come to look upon itself as possessing a definite entity. A good illustration is found at examination time when a class learns that a higher percentage of its students passed than in other groups. This feeling of class spirit is usually also generated when a class discovers that its individual grades are better than those in other classes. Indeed, a class will commonly take pride in even a single member's achievements. The students grin at one another and nod, taking satisfaction in their class's triumph. Two suggestions for improving the class image are:

1. Do all you can to increase the identification of each student with his class. For example, emphasize each individual's contribution in helping his class understand that day's lesson.

2. Seize every opportunity to praise the class *as a whole*. Such pat-on-the-backs as, "This is a splendid group," or, "I like the spirit of this class," will often bond its students into a solid unit. Generally speaking, group pressure is a tremendous force with teen-agers. Learn to use it to your advantage.

*10. The value of a "compartmented" approach for each class. How it can be obtained. Its importance to your emotional stabilization.*

We previously introduced the significance of your attitude. A "compartmented" approach means that you *look upon each class as a unit in itself.* The value of this attitude may become apparent when you realize that every class usually has its own characteristics. When you change classes, make it a rule not to take mental carry-overs of problems from one class to another. Generally speaking, worries from the previous class should not be held in the back of your mind while you are teaching the next class. Freedom from an accumulation of problems tends to stabilize your emotions—commonly considered advisable for a pleasant and successful completion of your daily program.

# CHAPTER 5
## For Better Class Control

### 1. The mistake of being too cordial with a class.

In an earlier section we dealt with some of the aspects of getting and maintaining control. It is such an important topic for a beginning teacher, however, that it is desirable to consider it in greater depth from the aspect of the class as a whole. One mistake sometimes made by inexperienced teachers is being overly familiar with students. The error usually springs from a mutual desire to be friendly and regarded by the students as a teacher who understands their needs, weaknesses, and ambitions. In itself the goal is worthy, but it should be established *on a basis of firm class control*. Indeed, curiously enough, as soon as you become "one of the boys," control frequently disappears and a breezy, back-slapping attitude often takes its place.

In most instances the adolescent mind generally has but two categories in school personages: teachers and students. When you attempt to be in both groups at the same time, you are usually asking for trouble. If you pose as one of the boys, nearly always their attitude is not to take orders. Instead, you often find yourself repeatedly asking them to stop talking, to pay closer attention, to do their homework, to bring texts as requested, to write down the assignment, to keep the place, or to turn around. Now you are their chum (chump would be a better word).

In addition, partiality is an almost inevitable charge. Some students are practically certain to mark your friendliness with other students as an indulgence that either they have less of or don't get at all. And favoritism is characteristically a cardinal sin in the teen-agers' world.

Thus in the end you are likely to receive the contempt of your class. Instead of appreciating your efforts, they may brand you as a weakling: you don't know how to control them and a good teacher would.

## 2. Should bright students run your class? A suggestion.

All classes have a mixture of personalities and abilities. As a consequence, an inexperienced teacher is frequently tempted to rely almost solely upon the more dynamic students to develop the lesson. If you do, within a short time you may find yourself helpless without their assistance. Also, when bright students become your crutch for putting the lesson across, your class tends to divide against itself. The less intelligent quickly say, "What's the use?" and usually sink into their seats. In a short time their minds ordinarily drift into a more-or-less organized unit whose chief purpose is to entertain themselves while the brains of the class hold forth. *Thus a group is formed that almost inevitably becomes a control problem.*

As a general rule the remedy is to pull both dull and bright into *every* question and discussion. A suggestion is that you first call on a student with limited ability, second, on one of average ability, and last, on the superior student to tie the presentation into a worthwhile contribution. Such a procedure tends to unify the class instead of disrupting it. Of course the pattern of pupil participation should definitely be varied so that it doesn't become obvious.

### 3. *Situations that may become booby traps in class control.*

Beware of situations that, by their nature, may make you reveal your inexperience in maintaining complete control. Examples are drilling for fire and air alarms, marching to assemblies, listening to an address by the principal. These situations sometimes take on the aspect of built-in booby traps. You have no class activities to help. You are not sheltered by the walls of your room. Indeed, you are usually in the spotlight. The eyes of the school are upon you.

It is frequently helpful if you take the precaution to make clear to your classes *before* these situations arise that they should have self-control, that their conduct is a reflection upon their citizenship, and that cooperation of everyone is necessary for the good of all.

As a rule your students know that they should maintain order. If there are violators, in most instances *deal firmly with them.* If in doubt as to what type of punishment, consult the supervisor in charge of discipline. Generally speaking, take advantage of his experience.

### 4. *Should you use downgrading as a punishment device? Its effect on control.*

If you lower a student's grades to punish him for poor conduct, you may injure the concept of self-control for the sake of character development. Possibly he may then erroneously think that your lesson is more important than his conduct and he may dislike your subject because you have used it as a whipping post. Putting it another way, you could scarcely expect much enthusiasm for your subject when it is used as a punishment for poor conduct.

There are teachers who maintain that no student should get a high grade if his behavior is unsatisfactory. But consider the following: When you lower a student's mark, let us say from 90 to 80, because he throws spitballs, you have clouded the issue. You are hiding behind your own inability to maintain necessary control. He should get his 90 and be given a separate rating for citizenship or a referral to the supervisor of discipline. Why not be honest? What is at fault is not his intelligence, but his citizenship. And that should be the basis of your punishment. In the final analysis, character training is of more importance than any subject.

### 5. Warning: He who hesitates loses control.

As a rule don't threaten secondary school teen-agers. It is usually a senseless gesture. They nearly always already know proper classroom behavior. Consequently, when they observe your hesitation, they may impose further willful behavior until an intolerable condition exists. In most instances the longer you hesitate to assert control, the greater your difficulties.

Of course it is important that you understand your class's problems and the troubles of a particular student. But it is also necessary that you be firm in administering control where needed. When you temporize, you are usually kidding yourself and everyone in your class knows it.

### 6. What do you do when your authority is challenged? Three basic procedures.

Sooner or later your authority probably will be challenged, bluntly and unmistakably. This is a painful moment. Usually you sense that the situation was building up to a climax. Sometimes, however, you have no idea that it is coming and are caught off guard. You stutter and stammer, gape in astonishment, or fly into a rage, depending upon your disposition. All are foolish but natural reactions. Calmly reading this page you nod your head and say, that is obvious. But what should you do? First, you ought to have an effective plan. Second, it should be ready for immediate use. Here are some basic procedures:

1. Many beginning teachers prefer to keep their troubles in their own backyard, if at all possible, feeling that handling their own problems proves to the class that they are fully competent. If you judge that you can handle the situation, try the following: "Charles, tonight I'm going to call your father. I think he should be made aware of your attitude." That evening, *without fail*, telephone. You'll usually get results.

2. If the situation is obviously more serious such a student should be dealt with *very* firmly but in private. When such a challenge to authority occurs, it constitutes the one situation where removing a student from the room may be justified. However, doing so should be avoided when possible. Have the student stand outside your room in the hall, by your door, or send him directly to the office of the supervisor of discipline, according to the established procedure in your school. After the class is over, you can deal with him privately.

3. It may be that in your particular school the previous procedure is not permitted. Usually such schools provide complaint cards that you send *immediately* to the discipline supervisor. Usually he comes promptly to your room to handle the situation. If your room is equipped with telephone service, you may be able to call him. Generally speaking, don't hesitate to use the card or telephone the first months of your teaching career if you deem it necessary. *Take advantage of expert help until you have enough experience to stand on your own feet.* Remember that sometimes poor control, more than any other factor, is the undoing of a beginning teacher.

### 7. What are you going to do about personal conversations? A suggestion.

As soon as you tolerate *some* personal conversations in your class, you almost automatically encourage more. Helen says to Irene that Joe is taking her to the movies next Saturday. Now Irene has to say something. She can't ignore Helen's secret or their friendship is ended. So she says back, just loud enough so the boys around her can hear, "Gee, that's swell. Wish I had a date." Charley catches on and ties in with, "How about going out with me?" Of course every student around them is listening. You probably don't have more than two thirds of the class's attention as a result of the one minor item of gossip. Worse, the ripple spreads across the class.

One way to deal with this problem is: Keep your eyes open, your ears alert for the *first* sign of anyone holding personal conversations. When it occurs, *stop the class.* Say, "Excuse me, just a minute—." Address the talker. "Do you want something? Can I help you? It must be important because you are interrupting our lesson. Surely you wouldn't do that unless it was absolutely necessary."

It is very helpful for good class control to insist that students pay close attention to the lesson. But we do need a caution regarding talking. Sometimes when students converse they are speaking about the topic under discussion. You cannot assume that *all* talking is personal conversation. In fact, the more interesting and controversial the topic of the lesson, the more the talk, and this can be an encouraging sign of a lively and successful discussion. To assume mere gossip at all times is generally not advisable. If you are alert, however, you can usually tell those who are genuinely participating from those who are holding personal conversations.

*8. Is there an undertone of seriousness? a respect for knowledge? How to engender these qualities.*

Another fundamental for establishing control in your class is the development of a serious attitude. Although touches of humor may be used, keep the dignity of your lesson. Each of your classes should have a respect for knowledge and a desire to master your subject. There are methods by which these qualities can be engendered. It is a mistake to believe that they "just happened." Indeed, they are usually carefully inculcated. You may find the following suggestions helpful.

1. Your mannerisms are often important. We spoke of this before, but at this point it needs to be emphasized again. You can scarcely expect a class to consider your lesson important if you show by gesture and tone of voice that you are indifferent. Furthermore, avoid personal peculiarities. For example, repeatedly pulling your nose or ear, or constant use of an expression such as, "And now—."

2. When one of your students doesn't understand a topic, take the trouble to have other students explain the difficulty to him. If this doesn't succeed, then you do so. If it still isn't clear, tell him to see you after class and you'll explain in more detail. It is generally advisable that each topic in your lesson be treated as important.

3. Make certain every member of your class has prepared his assignment. Frequently failure to prepare may indicate a disregard for your subject. This was mentioned previously, but it is worth repeating under this topic because of its importance toward developing a serious attitude. Of course failure to do an assignment does not always mean a disregard for the subject or the teacher. At this point we need to repeat some important questions: Does the student have a place at home to do the assignment? Has there been a family problem? Did the youngster understand the assignment? There are innumerable reasons why an assignment might not be done, and you ought to *diagnose before acting*.

4. Train your classes to have respect for the whole field of knowledge. Never "smear" another subject. All subjects make their contribution to our culture. Whenever opportunity offers in a lesson, refer to this basic concept so that the seed of genuine scholarship will take root. Strive to keep in sight your mission to broaden your students' horizons.

## 9. Politeness weaves a magic spell. But do you check on yourself? Four suggestions.

Politeness is amazingly effective in helping to establish control. For example, when a student is contributing to a lesson, make a point of requiring the class to listen out of courtesy, if nothing else, to what he has to say. Also, as mentioned in a previous topic, make it obvious that *you* are paying close attention. Don't twirl a pencil, jiggle keys, or stare out the window. These little signs are important. Remember that the class generally takes its cue from you. That is why you should constantly check on yourself. Actually, *you are almost always a part of the class— strive to remember it.*

Without making it obvious, train your class to overlook physical or mental handicaps of its members. The boy who usually makes a worthless comment because of his low mentality should be treated courteously. We could summarize the approaches as follows:

1. Expect students to be considerate of each other when contributions to the lesson are being made.

2. Defects in students such as baldness, deafness, stuttering, and lack of intelligence call for understanding. Generally speaking, it is surprising how sympathetically a class responds to students with handicaps.

3. Expect and demand courtesy from your students in their relationship to you.

4. Be careful of your own manners.

*10. The relationship between environment and control in the classroom. Two suggestions.*

The influence of the physical appearance of your room upon a class is frequently subtle but nearly always penetrating. When students enter your room they receive impressions. This is to be expected. But beginning teachers are not usually aware how important a contribution this can be toward good control. A room which has papers littering the floor, dirty piles of books tumbled on the teacher's desk, torn shades, and chalkboards covered with scrawlings from previous work is seldom going to put a class into the mood for crisp control. Your room should make two definite impressions:

1. It should be clean. No papers on the floor. The

chalkboards erased. Your desk in apple-pie order. Strive to have an unstained desk blotter. Have torn shades either repaired or taken down.

2. It should contain both an interesting bulletin board and an exhibition case. Your bulletin board should have live-wire items that change *daily*. *No stale stuff!* For challenging displays use color, neat lettering, plenty of large pictures or many specimens, and have a provocative title. If you share your room with other teachers, have your own display. Your exhibits, too, should be changed frequently for stimulation. Don't permit them to collect dust for weeks. As a rule make certain that your students make contributions so that they will take pride in what is being shown. Both the bulletin board and exhibition case should be *their* project under your supervision. Sometimes beginning teachers neglect to plan a time when students can see the material on display. Indeed, some teachers put material up for students to see but do not want students milling around the bulletin board and exhibition case—an obvious contradiction! You should allow a definite time for your students to participate in this important activity which helps to motivate them as to why the subject is worth studying. Perhaps a few minutes allotted each day at the beginning of the period is as good a time as any.

# CHAPTER 6

# *Suggestions on Miscellaneous Points*

## *1. The value of restraining your temper.*

The possibility is that if provocation lasts long enough, you may sometimes lose your temper, especially at the beginning of the term when you are reaching for control. Of course in some instances it may be necessary to let your classes know who is boss—a touch of the stitch-in-time philosophy put into practice.

But there are limits. You can't be constantly scolding your classes and expect them to respect you. Frequent emotional explosions disrupt classes. **GENERALLY YOUR AUTHORITY SHOULD BE ASSERTED WITH QUIET DIGNITY.** There is a borderline which you constantly watch. The deciding factor of exactly where this boundary begins and ends depends to some extent upon your disposition. Are you a hothead? Then cool yourself and watch your boiling point. Are you phlegmatic? The kick-me-again, I-don't-mind type? Then light a fire under yourself, or in some difficult schools your classes may run rough-shod over your control.

If you are like most of us, there may be times when you are unreasonable. When it is obvious, don't hesitate to apologize to your class. Simply say, "I'm sorry for being cross. I've got a lot of panther blood in me." They'll understand, laugh, and be with you once again. They'll know you're in the human group

—one of them. If you've bawled out a youngster undeservedly, apologize immediately in front of the class. This gives you the square-shooter approach and your teen-agers will love you for it.

On the other hand, if the class comes in ill-prepared, unruly, and antagonistic, put your foot down.

In summation: A beginning teacher should learn to match his temper against the classroom situation.

## 2. Physical emergencies and what to do.

During the day possibly 150 students pass in and out of your classroom. This means that by the end of the school year you had perhaps 20,000 or more contacts with pupils. It is reasonable to expect that some type of physical emergency is likely to take place. Consequently many schools have a set of instructions issued to each new teacher. In any event, you should have a definite, approved procedure.

For example, in cases where a student is injured, send *two* students to notify the office *immediately*. (Two students will corroborate that the message was delivered.) Stay with the patient until a school official arrives. *Statements must be written and signed by any witnesses, giving full details, date, and time.* These should be filed in the office with your report. In most schools there is a standard form for you to fill out. At times lawsuits are instituted against the city and/or teachers and you want all the facts on record.

Some students are subject to fainting, epileptic seizures, serious nosebleeding, vomiting, and so forth. In many schools guidance counselors warn the teachers. If you receive such a notice, find out *exactly* what procedure you should follow. Commonly the school nurse is to be notified promptly. A course in first-aid is required by some school systems, and teachers are expected to administer such aid when need is indicated. Certainly it is advisable to keep a first-aid manual in your desk.

In the event that a student is taken suddenly ill and

must leave the room at once, always send at least one student of the same sex along as an escort. Of course the matter should be immediately reported to the office. If in doubt as to how sick the student is, always assume a fully protective attitude for his benefit.

In hall patrol, lunchroom supervision, and auditorium assignments—*in fact at all times*—it is your duty to make a full report to the office of any accident *no matter how slight it may seem to you.*

### 3. Classroom mechanics. Nine suggestions. Make your room attractive.

We previously mentioned the importance of the appearance of your room under its influence on class control. Another significance is possibly its effect on you. There is usually a definite stimulation in having a trim workshop. When you walk into your room it is generally advisable to check on the following:

1. Windows opened properly for ventilation. Some schools have regulations regarding the bottom part of the window. Frequently either it is not to be opened at all, or only perhaps six inches, to prevent students leaning out. Use "weather judgment." Be careful if it is a cold day.

2. Shades should be drawn and raised carefully. (As previously suggested, torn shades should be removed. They give your room a shabby appearance.)

3. Chalkboards should be wiped after every class. Also, erasers and chalk tray should be cleaned each day. Make it a practice to wash the boards before classes begin. Chalk dust makes a generally messy condition.

4. The floor should have no papers on it. *It seems nothing makes so bad an impression so quickly as litter on the floor.* It may be helpful to assign any student caught dropping paper on the floor to the duty of picking up after his class. A suggestion is to have him report to you every day until the next careless one takes over.

5. Make it a habit to check that no papers are stuffed into the desks. Frequently they fall onto the floor.

6. Ordinarily train all classes to use the wastebasket `at the *end* of the period. It is not advisable to permit a student to bring up his scrap paper while the class is in session as that is often a disrupting influence.

7. As a rule there should be no bundles of old magazines, stacks of mimeograph paper, or piles of unused textbooks giving a disorderly appearance to your room. Sometimes this can be a problem when other teachers share your room, but do your best.

8. Usually keep an eye on your bulletin board. Don't permit torn displays to remain. Watch for scribbling on pictures.

9. Customarily make sure that the top of your desk is clean and neat. It is a prime example directly in front of your students.

For most of us it is probably advisable to have an established procedure to check on these mechanics. Before each class for the first few weeks glance quickly over the listed details. Your ability to maintain your room in excellent condition is sometimes taken as testimony of your professional attitude.

Of course you are not usually expected to be a janitor, nor does cleanliness and neatness have to be an obsession. Indeed, an excellent teacher may have an untidy desk and messy room. But in general a clean room and a neat desk is a good idea—it helps create the impression you want.

Ask yourself, "Is this a room I would enjoy entering? Does it look warm, inviting, interesting? Is it a place where people feel welcome? Are there plants around? Is the room sunny, colorful?

*4. The hazard of excessive paper work. Setting the pace. Is busywork ever justified?*

You may recall that in Chapter 3 we brought up the problem of written work and its burden on you. We are now ready to take up another aspect. Sometimes beginning teachers have difficulty in gauging the amount of paper work that is *essential*. Frequently there is no substitute for careful corrective paper evaluations that reward a student for his accomplishments. Generally speaking, your corrections should point out the weaknesses of a student to him so that he may improve himself. With this goal in mind, you should probe each class, searching for a student who needs help. *For this purpose written work is usually a valuable aid.* But, there is often the hazard of burying yourself under a mountain of papers. To avoid this, it is generally desirable to measure your ability to correct papers within a *one-day schedule.* Make it a general rule that *papers are to be returned next day.* So set your pace. One class at a time, or all classes together, but *return the papers promptly.* Don't make a meaningless gesture of giving written work that will not be handed back for weeks, if at all. Corrections are generally most helpful to students while the work is still fresh in their minds. Indeed, you should realize that the giving of written work is an implied contract between the students and you that it will be marked and returned to help them do better work.

Teachers sometimes give written classroom work to keep students occupied. A frequent device is having students copy related but not necessarily essential material from a textbook or the boards into their notebooks. It keeps the class busy, control is easy, and the teacher has nothing to do. *There is seldom an excuse for busywork.* If you are ill, but trying to finish the day, it is better to be honest with a class. Simply say, "Get your books out and do your homework. I need to catch my breath. I'm giving you a study period." Actually this situation probably wouldn't occur more than once or twice in a year, if then. Of course you should report to your subject supervisor what you did. In most instances he'll appreciate your professional integrity.

5. *The importance of writing a daily note about each class.*

You may find it helpful—especially at the beginning of the term —to write a note to yourself about each class at the end of every lesson. This procedure may enable you to locate weak spots quickly, for example:

First Period: Started very slowly.
Second Period: Lost interest toward end of lesson.
Third Period: Everyone enthusiastic except James Brown.

For practical purposes, keep your note in the classbook. When the class meets again, it may serve as a guide to help correct a situation. Thus, in the first period see that the lesson gets under way promptly. In the second period make certain that the lesson doesn't sag in its final stage. In the third period, speak to James Brown when he enters your room and ask him what went wrong during yesterday's lesson.

The daily note to yourself is a simple but usually effective device to keep both your classes and you on your toes.

### 6. Finding the best methods for teaching your classes.

You have a different personality from every other teacher. One way for you to find the best methods for *you* to help *your* classes is to experiment. Keep in mind that what is successful for another teacher—possibly even of the same subject—may not be advisable for you. In most instances your personality is an important factor. Furthermore, during your whole teaching career you should be constantly searching for fresh approaches and new ideas. Therefore, you may find it helpful to quickly develop the attitude of constantly trying different types of lessons, for example, the socialized discussion, the use of committees, the laboratory lesson for science teachers, and the pupil-project report. For the most part, don't be afraid that you might fail. The mere experience of striking out on a bold new front usually gives added strength to your approach to your classes. Indeed, the fact that you have this book in your hand tends to prove that you are on the right track. Keep at it. Strive to get ideas from many sources. You may find the following helpful.

1. Whenever possible observe experienced teachers who have an excellent record. As mentioned earlier, talk to them about teaching devices they have found effective. As a rule you will find them sympathetic to a beginner.

2. Study carefully the various methods that are suggested in books on creative teaching and try them. Keep track of the newest thinking on teaching.

3. Get helpful ideas from professional magazines. Subscriptions are generally inexpensive. This is a steady source of inspirational teaching.

4. Strive for original ideas. Use your imagination. Make a list of all the possible approaches you could use to present your topics. Usually you know your classes better than anyone else.

5. Take extension courses in nearby colleges or inservice training.

6. Attend professional association conferences, seminars, and demonstration lessons.

7. Confer with your supervisor after he observes your teaching.

8. Be willing to try experiments such as team teaching. For this you need permission from your supervisor.


*7. Be confident of yourself. Express your own personality.*


It is possible that you may feel in your first year or two of teaching that you are somewhat in the position of sink-or-swim. In most instances there usually is a vast difference between being a college student and a teacher yourself. So to speak, you have moved to the other side of the fence. Sometimes a beginning teacher has a sense of insecurity that reaches into his classroom when he stands before his students.

In the starting years of your career, you especially need a feeling of confidence in yourself. Possibly it is important that you realize most of us made mistakes and had to learn by experience—that we were all beginners at one time. Perhaps some of the ideas you had about the profession may need to be modified or even eliminated. We have tried to point out that usually you may need to adjust yourself to your particular teaching situation. Somehow, most schools seem different in various ways. So, it could be that confidence in your own ability will help to give you needed self-assurance.

Although you want suggestions from other teachers and fresh approaches from books on methods of presenting your subject, *express them through your own personality.* In most instances be positive in your attitude so that your classes feel you are sincere and competent in your efforts to help them.

### 8. What to do when you've pulled a boner.

We dealt briefly with this topic previously, but it may be worthwhile to consider it more fully at this point. Sometimes a beginning teacher tends to be considerably disturbed when he makes a mistake in front of his class. In this situation usually correct yourself as soon as you realize you've made an error. If a student raises his hand to correct you, give him credit for his alertness. Indeed, make a point of his contribution. It might be advisable to put a plus mark on his card. In addition to rewarding him, it may help train your classes to be alert to what you are saying.

Generally speaking, one of the worst blunders you can make is to pretend that you didn't make a mistake. For the most part, don't be upset because of your error, but on the other hand don't be indifferent. Remember that your students should look upon you as qualified to teach your subject. Incompetence in subject material is frequently one flaw in a teacher that many students in secondary schools may not overlook. A slip of the tongue, however, is a different matter. Students usually take it as a human failing and admire you for your willingness to admit it.

*9. The art of relaxed teaching. Five ways it can be obtained. Two of its benefits.*

In this topic we need to interweave some previous suggestions for a constructive approach. Relaxed teaching does not mean letting students do as they please, such as reading newspapers or magazines in class whenever they like, writing letters if they choose, or doing homework for other classes, or even the homework you assigned. Nor does it permit you to have an attitude of *I'm going over it once. That's all.* Such an outlook generally demonstrates callousness and nearly always arouses resentment. Another even more unfortunate approach is, *I don't care whether you fail. It's no skin off my bones.* The slower portion of your class commonly rebels against such an indifferent attitude. And skipping hit-or-miss through a lesson is rarely a solution because skimming is seldom advisable. Relaxed teaching is obtained as follows:

1. Strive to have control of your classes. When you have control, tension usually disappears.

2. Make it a rule to know your material thoroughly. This tends to give you confidence.

3. For practical purposes, commonly prepare your lesson plans diligently. Know approximately how much material you should be able to cover. The secret is *not to teach so much, but to teach it better.* Sometimes expressed by experienced teachers as, "The less in a lesson, the better the teaching."

4. Try to make sure that fundamentals are grasped. Once that takes place, you can generally be assured that rapid progress will be made. Consequently another source of nervousness tends to disappear.

5. Put yourself physically at ease. Walking *slowly* back and forth in front of the room helps. Move *quietly* down the aisles. *Casually* go to the sides of the room. But avoid pacing, like a tiger in a cage. *Relax!*

Relaxed teaching has two direct benefits: First, you are usually able to do better teaching throughout the entire day. It is frequently one of the first steps in successful teaching. Second, your classes usually feel a sense of security because they see you are at ease, confident they will do well.

### 10. How can you avoid getting your teaching technique into a rut?

It may be advisable to first make a list of all the various approaches you can find for putting across a lesson. This list should be steadily developed over the years and used as a reference for constant revitalization of your lesson. The challenge of working out different techniques should prove stimulating. You may be surprised how many approaches there are. Here are three examples:

1. *Pupil-run lesson.* Youngsters form a student-committee to plan, develop, and summarize a complete lesson under your supervision. (Object: Knits the class together.)

2. *Topics from Board.* Write a number of topics from the lesson on the board. Each student chooses the topic he wishes to discuss. First volunteers get the widest selection.
(Object: Makes an excellent review lesson.)

3. *Newspaper or magazine articles.* Clippings appropriate to the topic are brought in by students and discussed.
(Object: Provides a realistic motivation for developing a unit of work.)

Without much difficulty you should be able to expand your list into a couple of dozen procedures, giving needed variety. At this point you should realize that an excellent lesson plan helps to make your classes interested in their work. Also, as a consequence, control becomes less of a problem.

## 11. Changing attitudes at different secondary levels.

We previously mentioned the mixing of grade levels that might occur in your class. It may be helpful for you to understand the changing attitudes that occur as students mature. A secondary school teacher deals with young persons at what is ordinarily the most rapidly changing stage in their lives. Therefore, there is likely to be considerable difference in their attitudes at the various school levels. In the ninth grade, you usually find students exuberant, easily excited, and generally enthusiastic. By the twelfth grade, a considerable transformation has nearly always taken place. Seniors may look upon themselves as young adults and commonly think it sophisticated to have a bored attitude. The in-between stages of sophomores and juniors are adolescents going through extreme physical and social changes.

As a general rule, seniors should not be treated as freshmen, and juniors usually have changed outlooks since they were sophomores. If you teach both seniors and freshmen during the same term, you will commonly find a great difference between them. In dealing with freshmen you should customarily be direct and positive. Young teen-agers generally understand that type of leadership better than any other. Indeed, in junior high schools demand for the most part that they adhere to rules and regulations, even minor details. Seniors in a senior high school may be given considerably more latitude and self-expression. This is not to say that seniors don't need control. They do, but it should ordinarily stem from them as self-control rather than from you, the teacher. In addition, they have become socially conscious and the element of sex attraction enters the picture. Frequently dates and social events are of more importance to many seniors than any other activity in high school.

You may get used to handling only a certain grade of student, such as freshmen. When suddenly confronted in another term with seniors, your teaching probably will have to be altered considerably or you may have difficulty. Thoroughly understand that *each level in the secondary schools is equally important but they are usually different.* Learn to adjust yourself quickly to the level of each class. At the same time, realize that next term you may have students with very different horizons.

### 12. *Should you try to satisfy individual student needs within the class?*

Generally speaking, look upon your classes as being more important than any student while the class is in session. Of course if you are a sincere teacher, *you should be interested in every person in each of your classes.* Although individual needs are important, as a rule they should not be permitted to interfere with class time. Talk to a student before the class meets, at the end of the period, or at a time appointed for special counseling.

As a rule avoid having individual conversations while the class stands by twiddling its thumbs, an error that the inexperienced teacher is prone to make. Usually you can allow only a few words to an individual and then you should continue with the lesson. You could say, "Jimmy, you're not doing your job. Snap out of it. Get your work in tomorrow." If there are special ramifications and you wish to go into them with Jimmy, do so at the end of the period. Sometimes a beginning teacher becomes involved in a long, harassing argument with a student, and may leave the class without the instruction it is entitled to. This situation could resolve into a disrupting influence.

In the next section, we shall discuss suggestions to help you in your approach to the individual student and his problems.

*Section Two*

# YOUR STUDENT

*In the first section our major attention was upon
the class as a whole. We are now concerned more
especially with the students as individuals. Of necessity
there will be some overlapping and repetition, but
this may prove an advantage to beginning
teachers who want important points emphasized.*

# CHAPTER 7

# *Handling Troublemakers*

*Note:* Because the student is a part of your class, there naturally is considerable repetition of many suggestions from Section One, but now the emphasis will be on how they affect the individual.

Before following the recommendations made in this chapter and the next, you should circumspectly try to determine the *cause* of the student's behavior. The teen-ager may live in a broken home or with irresponsible parents. He may come from a large, underprivileged family in which he is the oldest child. He may have to take care of the house and younger children or work after school to help support the family.

**CAREFUL CONSIDERATION OF THE CAUSES FOR A DETRIMENTAL BEHAVIOR PATTERN SHOULD PRECEDE ANY AGGRESSIVE ACTION SUGGESTED IN THE EXAMPLES OF TROUBLEMAKERS WHICH FOLLOW.**

*Vigorous punitive measures should be reserved for only hard-core cases who have no legitimate excuse for their conduct.*

This material needs to be approached cautiously with a large question mark in your mind. A student who causes trouble may be a teen-ager who has troubles. Behavior is the *result* of some *cause*. Ask yourself, "Why is this youngster making trouble for me?" He is inviting trouble for himself and usually for a reason which, if understood, makes sense. Thus the advice as given in the following pages needs to be used with discrimination so that it does not lead to further delinquency. Remember you are primarily interested in helping the youngster, not in punishment.

### *1. The determined troublemaker. Six clues to watch for. Eleven suggestions to help you.*

One of the most difficult situations that an inexperienced teacher sometimes has to face is a student determined to be disorderly. You might think that every student would be especially considerate of a beginning teacher. In the select superior school this is largely so. Unfortunately, however, this is not always the case in every school. A few troublemakers seem to be sprinkled in the average school. Indeed, in difficult schools in problem areas a large proportion of a class may sometimes be composed of them. Frequently it is the aim of a troublemaker to arouse the entire class against you, to make a fool of you, if at all possible. Remember, generally speaking, he practiced for years in many classes on how to annoy teachers. He often takes pleasure in seeing you distraught and conscious of your inability to handle the situation he creates. More important than any lesson plan for that day is to uncover him and try to change his attitude *at the very beginning of the term*. In particular, if you have youngsters prone to misconduct in a difficult school watch for some of these clues:

1. Scraping of feet on the floor, or rapping of knuckles under the desk. Anything to make a disturbing noise.

2. Excessive hacking, coughing, and loud blowing of nose to draw attention.

3. Loud, boisterous laughter at the slightest pretext. Often accompanied by pounding on the desk.

4. Immediate and vociferous demanding of the lavatory pass. If it is refused, arguing about his right to have it.

5. Objects flipped across the room, especially pieces of chalk, clips, or paper airplanes. At the first opportunity he jumps out of his seat and loudly proclaims that someone is throwing things at him. Usually this is accompanied by loud guffaws from his pals.

6. The "stupid act." Can't find the page. Doesn't understand what you mean. Someone stole his homework. You are not talking loudly enough. Someone put gum on his seat. He can't read your writing on the board. His lunch is gone—it was there just a minute ago—he's hungry! Have you got an aspirin? And on and on.

Let us suppose you locate a troublemaker who is deliberately provoking a situation. What do you do? First, follow any instruction for disciplinary steps that have been issued by the supervisor of discipline. Second, keep in mind the basic suggestions made for establishing control in a class in the first chapter. To refresh your memory, here are some positive suggestions with additional comments:

1. At the end of the period talk to him privately. Let him know by the tone of your voice and your manner that you have no intention of tolerating his nonsense. *Be careful that you do not permit yourself to become involved in defending your actions to him.*

2. Change his seat to one directly in front of you. If he shows the slightest indication of getting out of line, speak to him in a low voice, as if you were his confidential friend warning him of trouble ahead. This technique often works magic, especially with younger teen-agers.

3. Make out a special disciplinary card that you keep in your files for future reference. Let the class as well as the troublemaker know that you are keeping a record. A variation of this technique is established in many schools by having an official blue or pink card made out that is sent to the discipline supervisor's office. A formal, carefully written complaint is frequently a strong deterrent to future outbursts.

4. Immediately send the troublemaker to your department office. Take the precaution to write a special pass *in ink*. Put the time when the pass is issued and request that the time

be noted when the student arrives in the office. The youngster is to wait there until the end of the period when you can go to thrash the matter out with him. This procedure has the advantage of getting the troublemaker out of your classroom so that you may proceed with your lesson.

5. If school regulations do not permit you to send him to the department office, keep him in your room, but have him stand in the rear away from supporting walls or desks. The gesture is that he is not considered a part of your class until disciplinary measures have been taken. A variation of this technique is to have him stand in the hall outside your room. Often, however, this last procedure is frowned upon by supervisors who feel that a student—especially if misbehaving—should always be under a teacher's observation.

6. Inform the guidance counselor. Be careful to give him an exact account. If possible, arrange a meeting with him, the troublemaker, and yourself.

7. Go to your subject supervisor. Usually he has the experience to be of definite help. In addition, he customarily wants his department to function smoothly. Of course be explicit in your charges.

8. Telephone to the parent, preferably the father in most cases, that evening. If there is no phone, and your supervisor doesn't object, write a letter *that afternoon* with a full account. Ask for the parent to see you in school to discuss the matter, stating the time when you have a free period. Cooperation of the home is important in disciplinary matters.

9. Contact the supervisor in charge of discipline. Be specific, giving *exact* and *all* details of your complaint. The completeness of your report is important because when the parent comes into school, the discipline supervisor will have your version at hand. You cannot expect him to support you if you file inaccurate reports.

10. In extreme cases, especially if there are indications of violence, send to the discipline supervisor's office for immediate help. Also, as soon as you perceive that the situation has slipped beyond your control, be careful of what you say and do.

11. On succeeding days keep a sharp eye on him. Call

on him frequently, but *don't bear a grudge.* Remind yourself that you are trying to correct a youngster's attitude, not persecute him. As soon as he begins to cooperate, ease up. Strive earnestly to work with him. If he makes a good contribution, praise him. The trite saying, "More flies are caught with honey than vinegar," applies here.

*Warning:* No matter how provoking the circumstances, do not attempt to maintain control by physical punishment. Hitting a student may have serious consequences: First, you may injure him. Second, you make yourself subject to lawsuit. Third, you become vulnerable for reprimand by school authorities. Fourth, you might get seriously injured.

The previous eleven suggestions are not given in any order of preference because the decision of what procedure you wish to follow depends upon your evaluation of how serious the situation is.

Stop the lesson *immediately* at the first indication of a disturbance in your class. Sometimes beginning teachers make the mistake of trying to brush by the situation. Generally speaking, to ignore a troublemaker is to encourage him to get bolder.

And don't battle him for the entire period. To do so usually solidifies him for an assault against you the next day.

Another word of advice: Don't threaten him with what you are going to do. Idle threats are seldom worth anything in correcting a determined troublemaker. In most instances proceed directly to whatever disciplinary steps you decide upon.

## 2. *The wise guys. They are a constant threat. Two suggestions.*

We sometimes have wise guys sprinkled into a class. They are not determined troublemakers, but they may be disruptive and can possibly ruin a class. They are typically on the lookout for an opportunity to make clever comments on a student's contribution or at something you say. Their purpose is to make the class laugh at or to someone's discomfort, and they are adept at doing just that. If you permit this conduct, they may actually disrupt the class and possibly you may lose some of your organized procedure. You may find the following advice helpful:

1. No smiles at their jokes and gibes. If you join in the ad-libbing, you can't expect much in the way of class control when you want it.

2. Normally make no friendly gestures toward these individuals. They are deliberately trying to undermine your security with the class.

Remember that *humor in its place is an essential ingredient* in a successful class, but it should always be under *your* control, not that of the wise guys who want to shine as class wits at your expense.

### 3. The outright delinquent. Caution needed here. Four suggestions to help you.

The delinquent teen-ager frequently presents a serious problem to a beginning teacher, especially in difficult schools. Probably you have had some training in this area through your courses in college, but the actual handling of a delinquent is a matter requiring both skill and caution. Some secondary schools have the services of personnel trained to manage this maladjusted youngster. Sometimes he is taken under the wing of a guidance counselor. Other times outside consultant services are available.

Very often the delinquent who appears in your class has already been in serious trouble, particularly if he is an upper classman. In fact it is common for a delinquent in high school to have been in children's court.

A beginning teacher should use extreme caution in dealing with this teen-ager. Experience is difficult to absorb secondhand and especially so in managing a delinquent. However, these suggestions may help you.

1. Keep close contact with all available sources for information about a delinquent. Take the trouble to know the whole story. Many of them are tragic and most of them pathetic.

2. Don't hesitate to ask for advice as to what steps to follow. Rely upon established procedures in your school. Two persons in particular will be helpful. First is the school disciplinarian, who almost always has had previous contact with the delinquent troubling you. In addition, the guidance counselor for that student will present his picture. These two opinions, supplemented by your own evaluation, may help to give you a basis for managing him.

3. You should understand that each delinquent usually presents a serious, complex problem and there seldom is an automatic, easy solution.

4. Some delinquents are expert at taking advantage of an inexperienced teacher, so be especially careful. In fact, occasionally a delinquent is vicious. This factor varies widely, of course, according to the particular school you are in.

*4. The teacher-hater. He looks upon you as the enemy. Four suggestions that will help solve this problem.*

The teacher-hater's attitude is possibly engendered by either direct or indirect experiences with teachers that left a sour taste. In all fairness we should admit that there are poor teachers. In fact, some are repulsive in their treatment of youngsters. Then, too, parents, because of embittering experiences, are sometimes responsible for instilling in their children the attitude that teachers as a group are not to be respected. These are unfortunate circumstances but they do occur.

The teacher-hater frequently exhibits himself as either a sulker or wrangler. If he sulks, he makes no contributions and any answers he gives are made as brief and inaudible as possible. If he is an arguer, he challenges every statement made whether he has justification or not. Either as a sulker or wrangler, he is often adept at involving a teacher in an altercation.

The following steps may assist you:

1. Never permit the student-versus-teacher attitude to develop.

2. Keep your good humor. Laughter is a valuable aid in this situation.

3. Make it obvious that the rest of the class gets along with you.

4. Be especially careful to be fair. Lean backward to make a point of it.

### 5. The dishonest student. Cheats. Lies. Forges notes. Five suggestions to help him.

Frequently the root of this student's trouble is fear. Sometimes he may be afraid that he might fail and be in disgrace at home. His classmates possibly will look upon him as inferior. His friends will probably abandon him. Even when appealed to on the basis that he is spoiling his character record, he commonly continues to cheat, lie, and forge absence notes.

But remember that if he cheats, he may care. That is an important factor. It is a possible assurance that you have something to work upon. Try to discover the *reason* for his action. Volunteer to help overcome his problem. The following procedures are often recommended:

1. Change his seat so that his temptation will be less.

2. Check his homework carefully to make sure it is original.

3. Have confidential talks with him, but make them to the point. Frequent brief conversations are usually much better than a harangue.

4. Trust him with his report card, but warn that you don't want him to "lose" it or forge his parent's signature.

(*Note:* If you find you can't rely upon his word, then send the card home by mail in an envelope with no return address. Sometimes a delinquent steals a second card, which is the one he shows at home. For this reason always keep spare report cards locked up.)

5. Tell him that his notes for absence must be genuine. Explain that you have his parents' signatures on file—and be sure that you do!

Let him know that he has to earn confidence. That once it is lost, it is not easy to regain, but that it can be done.

### 6. The truant. Five procedures to follow. Consider the class-cutter.

As a homeroom (also called register or section room) teacher, you deal with the truant as being absent from school. Nonattendance in your class, however, is a matter of cutting. Either case is a serious problem. Although affecting only a minority, it should be met with an established procedure. Different schools have different procedures, but in general the steps are as follows:

1. A notification is sent to the parent in a sealed letter. It should be mailed in an envelope without a return address so that the truant will not know it is a letter from the school and the parent will receive it. (Ordinary notification of absence is usually by post card on alternate days; thus, the first, third, and fifth absence when running consecutively.)

2. The attendance office in your school is notified promptly. Generally this is by a printed form for that purpose.

3. Frequently teachers are asked to phone the home and speak to the mother in cases of suspected truancy. If mother and father are working, then one of them should be notified at the business address. Truancy is a serious matter because it leads to delinquency. This should be explained to the parents when you phone them, whether at home or at business.

4. In extreme cases teachers are sometimes asked to make personal calls at the home. However, be sure to get your

principal's advice on this matter. Do not proceed on your own. In some communities home interviews of this sort are made by a qualified "visiting teacher."

5. In the case of a known truant, the first time he is absent *immediately* call the attention of the attendance officer to the fact.

The matter of truancy in secondary schools is so important that you should do everything that you can to prevent it.

One of the signs of truancy is in-and-out attendance. Thus a student reports for two days, is out the next day, comes back one day, is out the next. The following week is out two or three days again. The next week he may be out one day. *Spotty attendance is almost certain to be truancy.*

The other type of truant is usually one who drops out of school for a couple of weeks at a time waiting for the truant officers to catch up with him. When he is brought back to school he stays a few days, then disappears into the wild blue yonder. Such cases are commonly confirmed truants. Almost invariably they are waiting for a birthday to set them free from the yoke of compulsory attendance.

When the attendance officer returns his report, you should examine carefully the reasons for truancy. It is advisable to file such reports. In fact, most principals require that they be kept. Having a reference for previous absences will be valuable when you make out the next report on a suspected truant.

If a truant is in one of your classes, be careful of your attitude when he returns. Make sure that you reflect neither a sympathetic attitude, which may be interpreted by him as tacit approval, nor harsh treatment, which may be considered as justification for truancy. Let him know that you expect him to fall back into line. As a rule avoid mentioning the matter of his truancy in front of the class. Obviously in most cases this would be poor procedure. Naturally a truant would defend himself both by words and actions, and you probably would accomplish little or nothing. Strive to convince him that you want to help him respond reasonably to that which is reasonable.

And now a word about the class-cutter. The inexperienced teacher is especially likely to be deceived by him because of failure to check the daily attendance reports. Class-cutting should seldom be treated lightly. Usually it is symptomatic, customarily being accompanied by failure in your subject. The student sees no reason why he should continue to go to your class if he is failing anyhow. Unfortunately almost invariably the class-cutter develops into a truant, unless you take positive steps to prevent it.

7. *The pampered youngster. Eight features of the usual background. Four suggestions for correcting this situation.*

Behind the indulged student you frequently find a doting father or mother, or both. Sometimes the overindulgence is a form of parental pay-off for not really liking the youngster or not giving genuine attention to him. Almost invariably the roots of his trouble are in his family background. The question to ask is how can your school help him. Indeed, further rejection may be really very dangerous in some circumstances. Perhaps it is worthwhile to warn you that you seldom are thanked, but do your duty. The general earmark of the pampered teen-ager is that he often has a false sense of his importance built into his personality. Usually one or more of the following characteristics are evident:

1. Commonly his family is in the upper-middle or well-to-do bracket. His parents can afford to pamper him.

2. Sometimes the family is not financially well off, so he works but is allowed to spend all of his money on himself. Frequently he expresses his self-indulgence in fashionable clothing and a late-model car.

3. Often he has plenty of pocket money and likes to flash it. Frequently he opens his wallet to display a sheaf of five and ten dollar bills.

4. He commonly expresses the attitude that he is better

off than the teacher, so what you have to say can't amount to much. This frequently leads to a condescending mannerism which he likes to exhibit in front of the class.

5. Very often he is an only child, although not necessarily so. Sometimes he is a pampered grandchild.

6. He is likely to be good looking. In fact, he may be handsome. He has been told this so often that he is conceited.

7. Frequently he is a very bright person but does not measure to his ability.

8. Examination of his citizenship record on file in the office commonly reveals a history of many complaints by other teachers.

Although the indulged teen-ager is not the worst problem to an inexperienced teacher, he sometimes can develop into a prime nuisance that takes the joy out of life. Four suggestions that may enable you to make some inroad into this problem are: First, arrange for a conference with his parents. *The sooner in the term, the better.* The parents usually will not feel that you are showing built-up prejudice if you interview them at an early date. Admittedly, parental cooperation of such a student is frequently difficult to obtain. An he's-my-darling attitude has been developed for years. But try. Second, usually overlook nothing in your demands of this student. Generally speaking you are doing him a favor to make him toe the mark. Third, be on your guard for the possibility of a disrespectful attitude. Almost invariably he is a show-off. Fourth, be alert for excuses that he offers for poor work or for no work at all. He often has a slick tongue and frequently knows how to talk himself out of a difficult situation.

*8. The mentally unbalanced student who shouldn't be in your class, but is. Exhibits irresponsibility. The danger of violence. Cautions to follow.*

Although mentally unbalanced students should not be in the ordinary secondary school, we have to face the fact that sometimes they are. When evidence presents itself that you have such a student, of course you should go to the guidance counselor and find out what he knows about the case.

Examples of classifications that such students can sometimes be put into are:

1. Not violent but highly irresponsible. Manifested by a youngster repeatedly talking out whenever he feels like it, although the rest of the class is in complete order. Frequently it is obvious that he means no harm, but gets excited by a triviality.

*Caution:* *Select students who are calm and reliable to sit near him.*

2. Uncontrolled anger. When a student shows signs of becoming violent, be alert. He can become dangerous.

*Caution:* *There are certain subjects in which a student of this type should not be permitted.*

For example, in the chemical laboratory where concentrated acids and bases are available, or in shops where power equipment is used. In these areas any student given to violent outbursts is a hazard. Even in the regular classroom this student is a strain on the class and you. He should be admitted only when there is no proper facility to help him.

3. Extremely passive—even to the point of being uncommunicative. At times he is apathetic and ignores the entire class, frequently staring out the window at the sky. Although the acting-out youngster generally disturbs teachers more, the excessively withdrawn teen-ager may be far more seriously ill, yet is sometimes ignored by an inexperienced teacher.

*Caution:* *Do not take it upon yourself to label a youngster "mentally ill." The matter is very serious and should be reported in writing to your principal with details of any incidents and complete supporting evidence.*

## 9. An evaluation on control. Some cautions.

Care is needed that you—a beginning teacher—don't get a distorted evaluation of control. A misconception could stem from the concentration in this book on the problem control presents in some difficult secondary schools. It is commonly the most taxing single problem that many inexperienced teachers have to face in some areas of large cities. For them its importance is not to be minimized. But it is advisable, even so, that you do not get a distorted impression. Troublemakers, like criminals, represent a *very* small minority of the students. In preparing yourself for coping with problem teen-agers, don't have such a black picture that every day you enter your classroom with fear and trembling or, worse, with a chip on your shoulder ready to take on all comers. Frankly, *the control problem varies considerably from school to school,* and from one section of a state to another *even though only a few miles apart.* Furthermore, it is important to point out that the various types of problems described are *not* necessarily found in different teen-agers.

Strive to keep a positive attitude. Remember that your major goal is to develop the many worthwhile students in your classes. Assuredly you will find some students with great talents, many who are definitely bright, and *the vast majority hard working and conscientious.* They deserve your best efforts.

# CHAPTER 8

# *Understanding Other Problem Students*

*1. The slow student. He tries, but it's too much. How to ease his situation.*

As previously mentioned, slow students are often put into separate classes that may bear the designation "modified," "slow," "low achiever," "remedial," "retarded," and so forth. But frequently it is impossible to program such groups separately, and a slow student may appear in a regular class. Inasmuch as he usually cannot keep up with the material, you probably will quickly become aware of his limitation. For example, he is likely to be retarded in reading—some schools have special classes to help such a student in his reading deficiency. Bear in mind, however, that sometimes a student is not really slow but suffers from poor previous teaching or many other factors. Don't be too glib in labeling a youngster a "slow learner."

At first he commonly makes an effort to make good, hoping that this time things will be different. Because of this, inexperienced teachers sometimes do not recognize his difficulty at the beginning of the term. Usually he is older than the others in the class because of previous failures. Often he is conscious of his age, and it is one more unhappy factor in his situation. Sometimes he attempts to gloss over his inability with a gay mannerism.

You can frequently ease the situation for him by showing patience. Generally take the trouble to state your questions in simplified terms. And give him easy questions. More than that, sometimes help him with his answers. *Make him feel at ease in your class.*

A student with limited ability can possibly become a difficult problem if he is not handled with consideration. That is not to say that he should be passed even though he knows nothing about your subject. However, make every effort to understand his problem. Unfortunately many secondary schools do not have simplified programs for a slow student. Consequently he sometimes gets subjects that are difficult, if not impossible, for him to master. When you have a student manifestly incapable of passing your subject, it is your obligation to check with his guidance counselor *at the beginning of the term.* Indeed, you should check the previous record and achievement scores of *all* students in your classes at the start of the term so that you are conversant with their ability rather than wait until difficulties present themselves. For example, if you are teaching a subject such as physics, a student of restricted ability should not appear in your class. An error in programming may have been made. Perhaps he belongs in a modified physics course with only elementary concepts and limited achievements, and not at all qualifying for college entrance. However, even a large secondary school cannot as a rule offer a duplication of all courses on a modified level. In addition, program conflicts may force a slow student into a normal class.

### 2. Bright but troublesome. Suggestions that may help.

Offhand you might think that the gifted student presents no problem. Sometimes you couldn't be more wrong. By the time a talented student appears in secondary school, he may offer a challenge to the best teaching that can be done. He is possibly a future leader of our society, and an impetus should be given to his talents.

But he usually becomes bored in the average class and with ordinary teaching. For this reason subject supervisors commonly try to establish honor classes and give them to superior teachers. But, again, it is not always possible to make complete provision. As a consequence the brilliant student may appear in an average class. Unless you make a special effort he frequently becomes bored. In all fairness, he is sometimes already educated beyond what you are teaching the class and wishes, quite rightly, that he were out of it.

One of the best ways of tackling this situation is to challenge him constantly. Have students question him, dispute his statements, use every device to arouse his thinking. One suggestion is to have him work on special projects. Another suggestion is to make him give supplementary reports. *Keep him on his toes.* Too often an inexperienced teacher permits a bright student to sit idly by while the class works without his taking an active part. It is not a matter of giving him more homework. The emphasis should be on *quality,* not quantity.

### 3. The lackadaisical student. Five methods you can use to ignite a rocket under him.

First, find out why he is unmotivated. New teachers need to be warned about drawing hasty conclusions. For example, a student who works after school until midnight to help support a widowed mother is not a loafer. The lackadaisical student usually is a youngster who doesn't want to do any school work although he has no adequate explanation. He is generally capable, but he does not want to buckle down. He is a common occurrence among adolescents, particularly in the junior and senior grades. It is characteristic that he runs around the athletic field with tremendous vigor, but the moment he comes into your room he slouches into his seat and prepares to take his morning or afternoon nap. He reflects the attitude expressed in the scribbled messages, "In memory of those who died waiting for the bell," and "Bored of Education." These two quotations are sometimes scratched by him on his desk as an expression of his evaluation of school and its usefulness. In most instances approach him with a determination to motivate him into taking an active part in class discussions. As soon as he stretches for his siesta, put your questions to him. Keep up a running attack of asking him his opinions. Arouse his interest so that he has no desire to carve his messages of boredom.

Some methods that you may find helpful in stimulating his motivation and changing his attitude are:

1. The post card is frequently excellent. This procedure has been mentioned several times previously. Notify his parents whenever he takes the day off. Two or three post cards sent at the beginning of the term does an effective job. In addition it serves as a firm hint to possibly any other member of the class who needs a prodding to take active participation in the lesson. Of course its merits are restricted to the extent that parents are concerned.

2. A before-school session may also be helpful. Have him report for "extra stimulation." It needs to be only a matter of some ten minutes but it has tremendous nuisance value. You may have to give him a special pass to admit him into the building, but take the trouble to do so and be sure you collect it when he reports. A few of these sessions sometimes work like magic.

3. You can have him report to you after school instead of before. This is dynamite, not firecrackers, if he happens to be an athlete. You can be quite sure that his coach will not be happy about this arrangement, and if the young man is threatened with being thrown off the team, you will almost invariably get immediate results.

4. Special reports. These are often helpful for convincing him that he can do successful work. Let him select a topic from your subject that interests him. Offer him the opportunity to raise his grade by doing these special reports. Make the compositions short—say, three hundred words. As a result, he may get a more enthusiastic attitude toward your subject.

5. In most instances double check that he does all assigned work *on schedule*. It is usually helpful to let him know that you have no intention of permitting him to fail. Inform him

that in your class he has to work and you are determined to help him measure to his ability.

Dealing with a lackadaisical student usually requires positive action. You should strive to motivate him into an attitude of wanting to learn your subject. Uncorrected, he may destroy the spirit of enthusiasm which is vital to class success. As a general rule use the previous five suggestions in the form of a persistent attack that is initiated the moment you see him lolling in your classroom sun.

> *4. What steps should you take with the student who comes unprepared every day? Eight possible approaches.*

Here is a problem that sometimes is not limited to the student himself. You should consider him in the light of his failure to the class. The point often is, if he gets away without doing his homework, why can't others? Almost every person in the class is usually aware that this student is not preparing his work, and this awareness puts you in the spotlight. You have little choice but to do something about him. Often correction may present a difficult problem. Commonly it is not easy to convince him that he should bring in his work every day. Of course sometimes the home situation is such that doing homework is virtually impossible. Make it a rule to check carefully for this factor. Under ordinary circumstances, however, here are eight possible approaches:

1. Generally watch your attitude. Seldom convey to him that his failure to do assignments is a light matter. Usually this impression ought to be watched carefully.

2. It is frequently helpful to work on him. Talk to him each day as he enters the class. Watch for him as he comes down the hall. Yes, a nagging process sometimes brings results.

3. Often you can make arrangements with his guidance counselor to send for him for a consultation and possibly a reprimand.

4. It may be worthwhile to mail a letter to his parents. Explain the importance of doing homework regularly. In some instances ask that the letter be signed and returned to you. This procedure emphasizes its importance. As a follow-up, it may be advisable to telephone them every day he fails to bring in his homework. Become a pest if necessary but *don't let up on your pressure.*

5. Make it a rule that every day you give him the opportunity to redeem himself. During the lesson call on him. If he knows part of the answer, give him credit. Strive to make him realize that his contributions are important to the class. *Do not become discouraged.* Remember, frequently the entire class is involved in this problem.

6. If he becomes sullen and resentful, as sometimes happens in spite of your best efforts, take the matter up with the supervisor of discipline. Your attitude should be that there are no favorites. Everyone is expected to do his homework in your classes unless there is an unusually extenuating circumstance.

7. As a rule do not relent on your pressure. Customarily keep a steady, intense drive. It should serve, if nothing else, as an example to the class of your earnestness to help everyone.

8. Announce repeatedly to the class that you are, "Trying to get everyone to pass and get good marks." (As mentioned previously, this becomes your cheer-leader slogan.) Commonly it is your spirit that keeps your class on your side. Strive to make coming unprepared unpopular *with the class.*

In summary, your best approach is usually a sincere drive for honest work by everyone in your classes.

5. *How to handle the student who expects you to carry the whole load. The you-show-me-everything attitude.*

Sometimes a student sits back and looks at you as though you were about to perform the miracle of pouring information into his head. Sure, he's willing to receive. Aren't you willing to give? An agreeable teen-ager who wants to do right things. He is eager to pay attention but you do the work.

Usually it is a matter of attitude. For the most part this student has not been trained to study and get material for himself. Possibly somewhere along the line he has had teachers who have led him by the hand and drummed needed knowledge into him over and over. But at the secondary school level it is ordinarily advisable for a student to master the fundamentals of your subject largely by himself. Of course you should explain particularly difficult matter. But we are not referring to that.

In most instances train a student to do original thinking and to try to learn the content on his own. A freshman should prepare himself for the more difficult subjects that come in the junior and senior years. If an upper classman, he should realize that he will soon face an adult world and self-reliance is helpful for successful living.

In other words, in general don't permit him to rely upon you, if you can possibly avoid it. Try to keep your mouth closed as much as possible. Many beginning teachers do too much talking—a point previously mentioned. As a rule, let the student carry the weight of his lesson.

*6. The crude or vulgar youngster. Ways of helping him adjust to normal behavior. Three examples.*

There is seldom an excuse for a teacher to permit one of these individuals to express himself as he pleases. From the first day in your room it is ordinarily not advisable to tolerate any person expressing himself crudely or using vulgar mannerisms. In the main consider the atmosphere of your classroom. Generally speaking the crude or vulgar youngster is not often found in the superior school and not commonly in the average school: one tends to find him in difficult classes in an underprivileged urban area. In most cases he speaks out his crudities for the purpose of creating a disturbance. Instances of this might be as follows.

1. He makes a rude comment when a girl comes into the classroom as a messenger.

2. He mutters a vulgarity at a fellow student who displeases him.

3. At the slightest pretext he asserts himself in a crude manner.

Generally speaking your ability to handle this youngster depends a good deal upon your personality. You can place yourself in a precarious position by making inappropriate remarks to such a teen-ager. Indeed, sometimes he may come back with a wise crack which brings down the house at your expense. If the joke is on you—and fully proper—laugh with them! Develop the spirit that the class and you are one big family. This is frequently an effective method for helping him adjust to normal behavior. It is usually desirable that you give him the opportunity to express himself legitimately. Also, generally take the trouble to explain privately—after school preferably—to this youngster why it is important for his welfare that he develop good manners. As a beginning teacher, you may still have difficulty, even though you've talked to him a number of times. If so, it may help to take the matter up with his guidance counselor. If your difficulty continues, consult the supervisor of discipline.

We have repeatedly emphasized that your viewpoint should usually be centered on providing the means by which adolescents can become better adjusted to the adult life they are stepping into. When you run into a teen-ager who exhibits patterns of behavior that make situations difficult for him as well as others, make it a rule to seek every possible way of aiding him to solve his problem. *Be firm, but kind.* Try to make him understand that there are limits to what he is permitted to do. Take the trouble to explain that sometimes punishment is necessary in order to help him learn that as he grows into adulthood he cannot do whatever he pleases, when he pleases. Spell out why everyone should conform to the limits of permissive behavior imposed by society, whether in school or in the outside world.

Your task is not to "put him in his place," but to guide him into proper attitudes and conduct. Admittedly this is much easier to say than to accomplish, but strive to *keep it in mind.*

It is one of the things that frequently makes the difference between the superior teacher who is concerned about the welfare of his students and the ordinary one who thinks only of teaching his subject.

### 7. The jittery one. Signs to look for. Five suggestions for helping him.

The nervous adolescent is frequently a problem. Indeed, the presence of two or three jittery students in your class can sometimes be a serious matter. And it occasionally happens. It may be helpful to know what signs to look for. For example, some of them are:

    1. He laughs without apparent reason. Girls giggle.

    2. He gives an answer without being called upon. Sometimes he may shout it, although he didn't intend to.

    3. Physical manifestations: Bites his fingernails. Constantly runs his fingers through his hair. Absent-mindedly drums on his desk. Unconsciously makes faces at you or at the student speaking. He fidgets in his seat, back and forth, up and down, until you are positive the bottom of his pants must be worn to a frazzle.

    4. Class participation is an ordeal. He is painfully ill at ease. Frequently he stutters and stammers. He grins foolishly to cover his embarrassment. A girl blushes and closes her eyes.

Of course such a student deserves sympathy and you want to help him solve his problem as best you can. Here are a few suggestions:

    1. Don't treat him as a misconduct case. Unfortunately some teachers do this because they don't realize that his actions are the result of nervousness.

    2. Convince him that you are his friend. Show a sympathetic attitude when he contributes to the discussion.

    3. Try to remove his fear of failure. This may be the prime reason for his nervousness in many cases. Give him as-

surances of his ability. Tell him that he can do good work—with sincere praise for satisfactory responses.

4. Make sure that your class is with you in trying to help him. If necessary speak privately to a few individuals who don't understand the situation. Permit no laughter at him at any time. The students as a rule are considerate of his feelings, especially those in the junior and senior years.

5. Observe his normal reactions when he is talking to his friends before or after class. Almost invariably you may notice that usually he is not at all self-conscious and jittery. This is possibly the clue for your approach to help him. Often it is helpful to discuss this factor with him and point out that his nervousness may not be a matter of actual deficiency in him but of an attitude that he has developed in speaking before a class.

### 8. He lives in a daydream world. Four pointers to aid him.

This student usually does not pay attention to what is going on in class, yet at the same time he is generally not getting into mischief with other students. Frequently he leans upon his elbow and stares vacantly at the chalkboard, out the window, or possibly even at you. Now and then he hangs his head and stares at the desk as if looking into a crystal ball to see his future. He is not interested in what is going on because his mind is in the daydream world that the adolescent sometimes inhabits.

An inexperienced teacher may feel that this student is antagonistic. This is not necessarily so. He is customarily merely indifferent to the world the school authorities and you create for him. He wants to think about how it's going to be when he's older and got a good job, a snappy convertible, and a beautiful girl. Possibly one of the best approaches to his problem is through prodding him into keeping contact with your lesson. Don't be unpleasant but be firm and constant. Here are some pointers that may be helpful.

1. Keep pushing him with questions. Aim for frequent participation rather than a single competent contribution after which he is permitted to dream on.

2. Repeatedly ask his opinion about contributions made by other students. From this he may soon realize that he can't escape the class. Urge him to listen to what is being said.

3. Take the trouble to explain to him *at the end of class* that you are trying to help, not pick on him. It may be advisable to use this follow-up for the first week or so.

4. Promise that when he pays attention to what is going on in class, you won't have to call on him so often. This gives him a definite goal to strive for as a reward when he gets there. Obvious and simple, yet frequently effective.

*9. The lonesome one. Appears to have no friends. Sometimes deliberately shunned. Often a new student. Four ways to challenge the situation.*

You may notice that this student usually walks by himself when he comes into or leaves your room. He doesn't seem to join in as one of the class and it is apparent that he is not happy being with them. Sometimes it looks as if he is being avoided. Other times it seems that students try to become friendly but he rejects them. Report such cases to the guidance counselor for a thorough follow-up. There may be some serious implications. To meet the situation in class, try these approaches:

1. Speak to a few chosen members of the class who are capable of being friendly with him.

2. Make a point of talking to him before or after class. Ask him how he is getting along in class, keep talking about the class, speak of him as a part of the class. Tell him that you notice that he doesn't seem to join in with the class and ask him why. Search for an insight into his problem.

3. After class draw him into a brief *social* conversation with a member or so of the class. A school affair such as a dance, play, or game offers a legitimate excuse.

4. If possible repeatedly put him into a discussion group on some topic associated with material the class is studying. This activity will require his cooperation and sometimes gets him working with the class rather than sitting in his lonesome world.

*10. The hapless individual. Doesn't cover books, loses papers, forgets homework. Four effective ways to help him.*

Actually he is usually not a major problem. But you realize that he should become better organized. This student is commonly forgetting something. Undoubtedly he forgets to do his jobs at home. Even the things he wants to do for himself he forgets. Therefore, it is not a matter of being indifferent to you and your subject. And that is a consolation. Some ways to help him are:

1. Constantly check on him. He is disorganized, and you are doing him a favor when you remind him that he should measure up to routine requirements.

2. Have him write a reminder list. Ask him to show it to you every day. Have him put down whatever topics you desire. Check them off as they are done: homework, studying, special reports, and so forth.

3. Attach a minor penalty for each time he blunders. He'll catch on surprisingly fast.

4. Maintain a pleasant relationship. *Don't be nasty.* Most of us are well-meaning but hapless in one respect or another. Still, he should break the habit and change his attitude or he may get into increasing difficulties as he matures into adulthood.

Remember that in general the beginning of the term is usually the best time to tackle student problems because then the students do not have a built-up resentment towards you. At that time for the most part they feel you are entitled to be yourself, to express yourself, to demand what you want of them. After a few months they feel that you accepted them for what they were. A subtle shift in viewpoint, but a very important one.

# CHAPTER 9

# *More Problems*

*1. The teacher's pet. Six suggestions.*

Most of us have seen the teacher's pet in operation during our own school days. It is rather natural for the class to have possible resentment against him. Some of these suggestions may be helpful:

1. Make it a rule to beware of a rash evaluation of a particular student who dashes up at the beginning or end of the period and monopolizes your attention. It may be that he needs psychological reassurance more than anybody else. If you think this need may be evident, have a conference with his guidance counselor. The few minutes you have available at the beginning or end of the period are usually needed to establish cordial relations with all members of your class as well as for individual problems.

2. During the lesson itself normally present your material to the *entire* class. Remember that you are an important person to *every* student. Seldom make aside comments to particular individuals. Such a procedure of apparent favoritism may possibly arouse a resentment that you may not suspect.

3. As a general caution, be careful that you avoid a voice, gesture, or expression that may carry even a hint of favoritism. Inasmuch as students depend upon you for their grades and character evaluations, your bearing toward an individual is meaningful.

4. When a student expresses himself as liking you or your teaching, be on guard that you do not favor him either in his oral contributions or in marking his papers. Accept no excuses from him that you would not accept from another student, for example, late homework, no homework, tardiness to class, privilege of make-up examinations, forgotten book, misconduct. Make it a rule to be careful to check for facts, not who says them. It is normal to like those who admire us, and to fall into the error of favoritism is but being human. What makes it especially difficult is that almost invariably the student who expresses his admiration is sincere.

5. Have a helpful slogan: Friends with all, favoritism with none. Announce this philosophy repeatedly in all classes. It is usually especially worthwhile in the opening weeks of the term. Make it one of your ten commandments.

6. Tell your students that if anyone feels you are playing favorites, he is entitled to say so. Don't be afraid to meet the challenge. Examine it fairly. Teen-agers admire a teacher who is not afraid to face an issue.

*2. The lamb. Seven traits by which to recognize him. Five ways to help him be more expressive.*

The shy adolescent usually does not take part in class discussions and consequently in some instances is a problem. Commonly he isolates himself from work that requires group organization and cooperation. Many times he is a liability rather than an asset in class procedure. He often has a sense of insecurity that is frequently developed from one or more of the following traits:

1. He is afraid of not being accepted by the group. In self defense he sets himself apart.

2. He is afraid of being laughed at because he may give a silly answer.

3. He is convinced that he has odd mannerisms.

4. He is acutely aware of his physical appearance. His

ears stick out. His nose is too fat. He has long, dangling arms. He is too short and dumpy looking. Or some other physical feature makes him conscious that the group thinks him odd. Naturally he does not want to stand up in class and put it on display.

5. He is sensitive about his clothing, especially if he fancies that a certain attire is necessary to belong to the group. Girls in particular are sensitive on this matter.

6. He is generally more conscious of the overall picture of an insecure world than most other students.

7. On the few occasions when he speaks up it is usually a request for an additional explanation from you or for you to give him help in doing his work.

You can make the shy teen-ager more responsive by:

1. Realizing he is appreciative of approval. When he makes a contribution *praise him as much as you can.*

2. Having him work for *group* approval so that his sense of social inferiority may disappear, or at least be minimized.

3. Suggesting that he raise his hand and volunteer at least once each day. *Get him to feel that you are trying to help him overcome his difficulty.*

4. Urging him to join in the class discussion every day. Encourage his comments at different times during the lesson on successive days; for example, at the beginning of the period today, in the middle tomorrow, and toward the end the following day.

5. Extending an invitation to him, when special reports are given, to read at least part of his. Strive to make as many favorable remarks as possible.

3. *The scribbler and desk-carver. Five occasions to watch. A six-point check system that may help you.*

A desk-marker can be classified two ways. First, as one who uses ink to draw pictures, write his initials, or scribble messages. He is a nuisance and if not stopped may leave his desk a mess. Second, as a sculptor who enjoys carving. Many beginning teachers don't realize that his usual tool is the sharp point of the compass used in his geometry class. It digs deeply and gouges holes and long grooves that ruin a desk, often resulting in considerable expense for the maintenance department. Therefore, it is understandable that supervisors usually appreciate teachers who do not permit desks to be carved in their classrooms.

An examination of the situation frequently reveals that most of the scribbling and carving may be done by:

1. *Love-smitten.*   Names or initials of sweethearts joined forever by the pierced heart. A variation of this is the insignia of an ardent member of an athletic or social club.

2. *Absent-minded.*   Idly marks the desk while casually listening to the lesson.

3. *Finished the test and waiting.*   This student is killing time. He can't do any studying or active paper work. He has his pen in hand from taking the test, and so he begins marking the desk while waiting for other students to finish. Quite common and not to be overlooked, but at the same time not so deliberate.

4. *Bored.*   He is not interested in the lesson at all. You won't let him fly airplanes around the room. He can't sing, hum, or dance a jig, so what is he to do? Well, he can write messages on his desk to someone who may be sitting there the next period, or he can get out his knife and do some sculpturing to entertain himself.

5. *Deliberate.*   This youngster is almost invariably a failing student who wishes to leave some memento of himself in a school where he spent so many wearisome hours. Usually he carves deep and wide.

You should realize how quickly the disfiguring of desks is frequently accomplished. In difficult schools where misconduct is a serious problem, unless you take the trouble to maintain constant supervision, the desks are almost certain to be marked and scarred. Furthermore, if your room is shared by other teachers and their classes, the matter possibly becomes more difficult. But as a general rule, all teachers work together on this problem. If you are in a school where the marking and scarring of desks is a problem, a check system that may help you is:

1. Take the trouble to make a *daily* inspection at the end of each class. Examine all desks carefully. It will take only a minute of your time but is well worth it. The next day you greet offenders and demand an on-the-spot explanation.

2. Keep your eyes open during the lesson to make sure no one is marking a desk. Especially be aware of the student twirling a compass in his hand, or idly holding a pen.

3. Have monitors who inspect desks for each row. Do this in each class. An easy system is to make the last person in each row automatically the monitor. He checks each seat in his row as he leaves the room every day. Whenever a desk is marked, he immediately reports it.

4. A student checks his own desk when he *first* enters your room every day. He promptly lets you know of any marking or carving. This pin-points the offender as being the person who occupied that seat in the previous class.

5. Announce that parents are financially responsible for acts of their children. That a penalty will be collected for refinishing or getting a new desk, whichever is deemed necessary. Push the point even though local ordinances vary as to extent of legal liability. You will probably receive support from your principal as he is generally anxious to protect school property. However, it is advisable to check with him to be certain you have his approval. Cooperate with the discipline supervisor and the custodian in having a mutilated desk refinished or have the parent pay the penalty (about three dollars in New York City). The fact that parents may have to pay for any damage done to a desk is usually a very deterring factor except for the pampered youngster from well-to-do families.

6. Have a rigid penalty system and customarily enforce it. In most instances anyone marking a desk with ink should scrub it off that day. Keep a can of scouring powder and cloth in your room so that immediate correction can be imposed. The message ordinarily spreads far and wide. If carving was done, the student should bring in sandpaper, wood filler, shellac, varnish, and brushes. He should do the desk to your complete satisfaction

at the end of the following school day. Generally speaking make a definite example out of it. Next day in all classes point to the desk that was done over. This is practically sure-cure. It often brings amazing results. Usually there will be no more scarring of desks in your room.

Success in this, as in so many other control measures, is to get your procedures established *at the very beginning of the term.* Control is a prime factor for teaching success and desk marking is a typical example of where you can firmly entrench your standards *from the first day you meet your class.*

### 4. The physically handicapped. Four aspects of the problem. Five ways to help this student.

A beginning teacher may not expect that a problem may arise because of a student's physical handicap. At times, however, such disabilities as poor sight, faulty hearing, baldness, deformed hands or legs, or impaired speech may cause one of the following situations with a student:

1. He may not pay attention because he believes he won't amount to much anyhow. Success in life is not for him.

2. He believes he is on display, that everyone thinks he is a freak.

3. He is convinced he is not attractive to the opposite sex. As an adolescent, this is a crushing blow.

4. He feels that his fellow teen-agers will never accept him as one of them. Certainly they will not hold him in high esteem or choose him as a leader.

Some ways to help this student are:

1. Have a series of "Dutch-uncle" talks with him. Point out that success is a relative term, that there are different types of accomplishment, that many men have overcome great obstacles.

2. Emphasize that we are all on exhibition with our faults, that life is unfair to most of us in one way or another, that many people have handicaps in mental disability that are more serious than physical disadvantages.

3. Convince him that there are compensations in life for those who do not get married, and that sex attraction is not limited to the handsome and beautiful, that the communion between man and woman is more spiritual than physical if it is to last, and that many handicapped individuals marry.

4. Explain that he will have to work to earn the esteem of his fellows. If he deliberately rules them out of his life, he can scarcely expect them to look upon him as a leader.

5. Of course you should make necessary adjustments to help him. This could include such things as seating for sight and auditory disabilities, consideration for stammering and stuttering, and understanding for psychological idiosyncrasies like the intelligent student who can't read or spell. Expand yourself to be sympathetic with his needs.

*5. He's usually late to class. Seven steps you can take to teach him to be prompt.*

As you might expect, it is almost always the same student who is late. As a rule don't make the mistake of ignoring his lateness or passing it over lightly. If you do, the habit of being late may spread rapidly through your class. Remember that a teen-ager, especially if prone to misconduct, is usually alert to any dent in a beginning teacher's control.

When a student is late, commonly make a note of it. It is advisable to ask him to report at the end of the period when you can get a full explanation. Also, it is frequently helpful to let him know that you keep a careful record of any lateness. Thus you would say, "This is your third lateness, Charles. See me at the end of class." In this manner you generally avoid a situation which can disrupt your class, but at the same time the impression is normally made that lateness will not be tolerated. When the dismissal bell rings, find out why Charles was late. However, be sure you don't detain him too long. You don't want to make him late for his next class.

Assume the general attitude that you are reasonable if there is a legitimate excuse for a lateness but you expect a satisfactory explanation.

The following steps may prove helpful in dealing with lateness:

1. Check the student's program to see where he was the previous period. In many schools a student is required to carry his program with him at all times so that this will be a simple matter. If he has to come from the gym, climb four flights, and go to the opposite end of the building within three minutes, it is reasonable that he would be a moment or two late. It is only fair that you take these factors into consideration.

2. Sometimes unusual traffic jams occur in hallways. If you get such an alibi, investigate it, and if such a situation persists try to have it removed. The point here is that, again, you want to be fair to the student.

3. Explain to every late student that lateness is a discourtesy to his class and to you. Consequently, it is to be avoided if at all possible.

4. Lateness may disrupt the class and sometimes interferes with its progress. Explain this to the person who is late and let him know that is why you cannot tolerate his being deliberately late to your class.

5. Explain to a late student that he loses something by not being in your room at the beginning of the period. Emphasize this by:

a. Starting your class very promptly—*at the bell.*
b. Making sure that something worthwhile is done in the first minute of the period.

6. Keep a careful record. The first time a student is late, warn him both at the beginning and end of the period. The second time, hold a brief conference at the end of the period. Go into the factors that caused a repetition of his lateness. Explain in detail why his lateness in getting to your class is serious. The third time, if it is obvious that he is negligent, punishment is in order. An effective device is to have him report to you after school

for five minutes—*but not if it makes him miss the only school bus he can get.* Five minutes is not much in time and should not inconvenience you to any considerable degree, but it gets the point across and is remarkably effective. In the event he must take the school bus, then telephone the parents that evening.

7. If lateness still continues, it is a matter to take up with the supervisor of discipline.

In most instances, make an issue out of lateness. Don't look upon it as a matter of a student or so coming in a minute or two late. Continued unexcused lateness is a minor infraction, but it reflects the student's attitude toward his class.

*6. The excessively absent student. Two types leading to a control problem. Four suggestions.*

When a student is absent a great deal, he usually falls behind in his work. The next step is that he frequently loses interest in what his class is doing. Consequently, he may become bored and a control problem possibly develops. We can generally classify excessively absent students into two groups:

1. A single long absence in which there is an important loss of accomplishment. This type is usually caused by serious illness.

2. An in-and-out absence over a long time that is disruptive, but still carries a thread of what is going on in the class— commonly a matter of truancy.

Some suggestions which may prove helpful are:

1. When poor attendance is caused by illness, mail the assignments for the student's class to his home as soon as you receive word he is convalescing. This encouragement helps him to keep up.

2. When he returns go easy on him the first few days. But let him know that by the end of possibly a week you expect him to be generally in line with the rest of his class. A week is usually sufficient time, but naturally the amount of time you allow

him varies with the length of his illness. But as a rule establish a definite goal by a definite time.

3. In Chapter 7 we mentioned the excessively absent student when considering the truant. We should admit that he frequently presents a difficult problem if he is counting the days to his release from school. If you know that he is going to be discharged within a few weeks, usually the most you can expect is that he be quiet and orderly so as not to create control problems. Be frank with him. It is generally helpful to tell him that good behavior is all you expect, and permit him to bring a suitable book to read or have a book for him to read each day he appears in your class. The area of common sense should prevail here. Remember, usually the welfare of the class comes first.

4. If the truant is not going to be discharged, then as a rule proceed to instruct him as a regular member of the class, striving to make him pass if you possibly can. If you succeed, he may change his mind about being a truant.

*7. The "carry-over" problem student. Three examples of sources. Three suggestions on how to handle this situation.*

We previously dealt with the class that enters your room in a no-work mood, but you should realize that all students tend to bring some effects of the previous period they were in. If that teacher had excellent control, you may receive the benefit when his students come into your room. There are, however, places where students are permitted to become boisterous. If a student comes from one of these, you sometimes have a carry-over problem in control. Three examples are:

1. If the previous period was for lunch, there is, of course, the freedom to laugh, talk, and move around. This is as it should be. Students need a time for relaxation and social contacts.

2. In health education there are games with freedom of shouting, laughing, talking, running around. Like the lunch

period, this provides needed relaxation and, in addition, exercise.

3. The first two groups are necessary for a balanced program. But the carry-over problem of a student from a class that has poor control and that immediately precedes your class is frequently a different matter. Unfortunately all teachers do not have excellent control over their students. Indeed, in some classes control may be more noted by its absence than its presence.

Teen-agers are usually extremely responsive to a mood. Sometimes an entire class can easily become affected by the conduct of a single member. Although we have already dealt quite exhaustively with the handling of control problems, the topic is so important in some difficult schools that three suggestions possibly warrant repetition at this point—in case you have classes where conduct is a problem. Thus, a helpful procedure may be as follows:

1. Note which student in particular is causing trouble. After that, keep your eye on him from the *very beginning* of the period. As a general rule a student needing control has to learn where and what the limits of permissibility are, and that punishment sometimes has to be employed to help him learn what those limits are.

2. Have *brief* conferences at the end of the period. Explain that when a student comes from lunch, gym, or another teacher, he has to *leave the past period behind him*. He gets a fresh start in your room. Explain that he should conform to your standards in your class.

3. Next day at the beginning of the period stand *at the door to your room*. When the student who presented a problem the previous day comes along, make a point of greeting him *before* he goes through the doorway. Check that he is in a proper frame of mind to respond to the control you want. If he is not, talk to him. Remember, the mood of a youngster is extremely important.

*When you have a problem in control, usually think of your student in terms of an individual needing private instruction. Generally approach him as an isolated behavior case, following the principle of divide and conquer.*

8. *The underprivileged student. Four methods of dealing with him compassionately, yet firmly.*

The percentage of underprivileged students who appear in your classes varies considerably with the neighborhood surrounding your school. It is important to realize that *many of these students have their happiest hours in school.* They look upon school as a place where they can escape from the backgrounds that trap them. Also, remember that school is their opportunity to improve themselves. Even though they may not be making the progress you want, they are accomplishing a great deal. Almost every teacher who has to deal with underprivileged adolescents soon realizes the challenging responsibility he has. The handicaps of limited income, alcoholic parents, broken homes, constant quarreling, immoral conditions, overcrowded living quarters, loss of a parent, and so forth, work themselves into ugly combinations against these teen-agers. In some cases we have to add the factor of limited intelligence, and such adolescents may face an unhappy future. Life can easily become an intense struggle or even tragic for them. A chip-on-the-shoulder attitude is sometimes to be expected. Frequently it is not easy to penetrate the hard shell with which many of these teen-agers surround themselves. Under such circumstances, it is not surprising that some of them may become juvenile delinquents.

Try to have the judgment and patience necessary to understand the handicap under which they may be attempting to do their school work. Here are some methods for dealing compassionately, yet firmly, with them:

1. Make it a rule to take into consideration the student's difficulties. This does not mean that he can use his circumstances as an excuse for doing no work, but you should have a large measure of understanding. *Poor work from him may be more difficult to obtain than good work from another student.*

2. In most instances don't meddle in a family situation. Ordinarily this is not your province beyond the fact that you should report evidence which has come to your attention to the

guidance counselor, social worker, and the supervisors so that there may be a better understanding of this student and his problems. A home visit, under such circumstances, generally should not be undertaken unless recommended by some school official.

3. Don't hesitate to use as much praise as you possibly can squeeze out for this student. He needs encouragement. It is up to you to help him every way that you can.

4. Strive to express your interest in his future. When opportunity offers ask what his plans are after he graduates. By talking with him you sometimes unearth a sad, hopeless attitude or an ambition totally out of line with his ability. For example, a boy with a low intelligence rating, a poor achievement record, inferior potential scores, and no money, is not in a position to support the ambition of going through medical college or becoming a nuclear physicist. Don't feed impossible dreams. Help him in a realistic manner.

### 9. *The student with a crush on you. Five suggestions to ease the situation.*

As a young teacher you may be no more than four to six years older than the students in your classes—especially if they are seniors. The fact that you are slightly older sometimes represents sophisticated romance to a teen-ager. Some suggestions to make the necessary adjustments are:

1. Do not remain in your room alone with this student. Step into the hall or at least into the doorway.

2. Make a point of having your door open after the class leaves, particularly if this student lingers in your room.

3. Have an excuse to get rid of this student. Be polite but firm. Say, "I'm sorry but I can't chat. There's another class coming in." Or, "I've got reports that must be done immediately." Or go some place for a "conference."

4. Avoid personal discussions. This avenue sometimes leads to trouble. *Avoid any semblance of boon companionship.* On

occasion, however, personal talks can be used to "clear the air."

5. Frequently these situations develop before you realize what is happening. As soon as you are aware that a student has a crush on you, break it off without hesitation, yet without hurting his or her feelings.

> *10. Minor infractions. A nuisance rather than serious, they can still be troublesome. Some examples.*

Lesser infractions disturb you more or less according to your temperament. In addition, your school may have stricter regulations on some minor matters than other schools have. A few examples are:

1. *Chewing gum.* Some teachers consider this rather important and others, on the contrary, look upon it as a matter of release of tension that may be present in the student. Some principals are strict about it, whereas others are not much concerned.

2. *Eating in class.* Sometimes students open their lunch bags and start nibbling on sandwiches. This can be disconcerting and generally is not approved. However, when a student attends a very early class (as in a crowded school on double session) and has a long time before lunch, you may feel that the student's nibbling is somewhat justified. This is, of course, subject to your principal's attitude.

3. *Combing hair.* Can be quite a nuisance in some classes. Girls particularly are apt to make it an elaborate activity. Some supervisors don't mind if combing is done in homerooms (register or section rooms), but almost invariably it is not permitted in class. It is easy to stop by having combs put away the moment they appear. It is not necessary to confiscate them. Taking a student's property, even for a short time, sometimes builds resentment in the adolescent.

4. *Other minor infractions.* There are numerous small

problems that may disturb you. For example, passing of notes between youngsters, snatching another student's books and handing them around the room, grabbing someone's lunch and hiding it in a desk, and so forth. This nonsense should seldom be permitted. Repeatedly point out that these are children's games. That usually stops these antics.

The matter of misconduct in minor infractions is one which you should keep your eye on in terms of relative importance. Do not take the same attitude toward a teen-ager who openly defies you that you do for the student who accidentally drops his pen on the floor. Use judgment. Try not to distort a situation— a common tendency for inexperienced teachers. Furthermore, remember that *maintaining control should not be a matter of how you feel at the moment*. Even when you and your class are laughing at a humorous incident, your control should be both positive and evident.

### 11. The importance of inherent motivation in dealing with problem students.

The desire to learn aroused within students is an extremely vital factor in overcoming behavior problems. In this section we concentrated on devices that should help you in an immediate situation, but it ought to be clear that they are to be used only after you have done all you can to make your subject interesting and to capture the attention of your students by careful planning of motivational experiences. Motivation in your daily lesson will help you to maintain control. If you convince your students that they are learning something worthwhile, you have the key to unlock problems that may present themselves in your classroom.

### 12. Summation.

This whole section on student misbehavior and problems does not pretend to have psychological depth. For that, you should do careful supplementary reading of recognized texts. Some books are on the suggested reading list at the end of this handbook, other recommendations can be easily obtained. As a rule be highly critical of snap judgments and generally punitive and rejecting attitudes. If student behavior is not good, don't judge the youngster as necessarily "bad." Be careful not to get that impression from our discussion of problems with teen-agers. Because we are striving to be helpful with specific examples you may get an unbalanced negative view. Indeed, one of the risks of a book of this type is that the apprehensive beginner is apt to feel overwhelmed by the problems with which it confronts him.

*The average youngster in the average school presents little or no problem*—still, it is helpful to be prepared for the occasional troublesome difficulty.

# Section Three
# YOUR ATTITUDE

*Your attitude toward the teaching profession will be
an important factor in your success or failure. Resist
the tendency to form an assembly-line approach where
students are considered as so many teachable units.
You may well be the source of inspiration. The
run-of-the-mill student who becomes Mr. Average Man
remembers the teachers who thought him important
enough to give him personal attention. The biographies
of great men are replete with references to teachers
who vitally affected their lives by instilling personal
standards and a firm attitude toward sincere
scholarship. Thus control for its own sake has restricted
significance, but it is the platform upon which respect
and dedication are built. Let your attitude reflect
your devotion toward helping your students to attain
the larger goals of living.*

# CHAPTER 10

# *Attitudes for a Constructive Outlook*

*Note:* At the end of the previous chapter we cautioned the beginning teacher not to think that all teen-agers are behavior problems nor that keeping classroom control is generally extremely difficult. Individual behavior and classroom control are not usually serious problems under ordinary circumstances. Unfortunately the repetition of problems considered in different aspects in the following chapters tends to emphasize the problems out of their generally true perspective. But this handbook is designed to guide you through difficulties, and so repetition to some extent in the following chapters is largely unavoidable if a rounded picture of a particular problem is to be presented. Remember, the problem itself may not occur during your probationary period; but if it does, you may find a suggestion to help you. At that time your attitude may prove important and a single helpful suggestion on how to handle a negative situation may prove very worthwhile.

*1. The analytical approach. Five methods for developing better perceptions.*

An analytical approach may help you avoid blurred concepts about school situations. Here are some suggestions.

1. Strive to formulate a definite standard of values. Try to know what moral, spiritual, and educational goals you are striving for. Admittedly experience helps, but often even a novice who has positive aims has more discernment than a teacher who has been dragging his feet for years. Of course sometimes you cannot set definite standards for some kinds of situations because these may not be known to you. Indeed, frequently you may arrive at only an approximation of what is adequate. After much experience, even this may shift and alter as persons and times change. But as a general rule you may find it helpful to set your goals with the expectation that experience may modify them.

2. Try not to repeat your mistakes. We all make errors, but analyze what it was that you did wrong. The important thing is, don't make the same mistake again and again.

3. Train yourself to think ahead. This is particularly important for keeping on schedule, getting clerical reports in on time, being prepared for department and faculty meetings, and so forth.

4. Study how to handle situations. The purpose of this book is to give you definite assistance in many types of problems even at the risk of repeating some previous advice and possibly overdrawing some of the material. Use it as a guide for constant reference. In addition, *get viewpoints from other sources.*

5. Develop a constructive outlook. Your achievement will seldom be total. You can only do the best that you are able. But it is important to try to reach your best, and analytical thinking can help you to make such progress.

>    2. *Know your limitations. Your measured view-point.*

As a conscientious teacher you may often have a sense of frustration. You want to help all of your students every way possible but feel that at times you fail them. It may be helpful to realize that you are but one cog of the wheel. You are an important part, to be sure, but not the beginning and end of the educational system.

You catch a student and hold him for a moment, then thrust him forward—a definite contribution, but with limitations. Don't permit yourself to become overwhelmed with discouragement because you see the many opportunities at hand and realize your shortcomings. In other words, in general have a measured viewpoint of what can be obtained and how you can reach that goal. You are not a psychologist or psychiatrist. Nor are you the principal. You are neither mother nor father to all your brood. Nor are you their buddy. Rather, you are a little bit of all of these plus much more that only a *teacher* can fulfill.

### 3. *Your attitude toward emotional stress. Three goals.*

Teen-agers characteristically have tremendous possibilities for sometimes suddenly rolling out of bounds, so adjust your mind to expect some possible trouble during the day. On the other hand, tend to be confident that you can control whatever situation may arise, but don't exaggerate or minimize it. Strive to *develop a sense of the relative importance of matters.* In general *cultivate and maintain an attitude of calm, sure procedure.* Remind yourself that at times the adolescent is unbelievably incapable of evaluating what is important and what is trivial. Consider these goals:

1. *A sympathetic heart.* Occasions arise in which a student needs an older person to guide him over a rough spot.

2. *An understanding ear.* It is often the better part of judgment not to hear everything that is wrong. *Learn to develop tact,* one of the most important traits a secondary teacher needs.

3. *A benevolent eye.* Why see all faults? An adolescent usually doesn't mind correction but if he feels that he makes nothing but mistakes, that he is incompetent, he becomes discouraged. In some instances he may not have the necessary stamina to struggle on. *When you convince a teen-ager he is hopeless, you create a problem that has widespread repercussions.*

Do not confuse a sympathetic heart, an understanding ear, and a benevolent eye with an everything-goes attitude toward behavior. Curiously, students usually want their teachers to make them measure up to good conduct, yet be sympathetic for academic shortcomings. Nearly always be generous in prasing a teenager for his accomplishments, give the best marks that you can, and strive to limit your corrections. It is usually recognized that this attitude lessens emotional stress and promotes high scholastic achievements because you win the confidence and cooperation of the adolescent.

### 4. *Your attitude toward your mastery of your subject. Four points to consider.*

Mastery of your major subject is vital in secondary schools. Strive to keep yourself informed of the latest techniques and advancements. The following points emphasize the importance of thoroughly knowing your material:

1. *Your student.* Your scholastic background tends to seep through in every lesson. In no time at all, your students seem to know whether you are accomplished in your subject, skimming by, or a fake.

2. *Your department.* In contact with other teachers of your subject, many occasions may arise in which your knowledge is revealed. The making and marking of examinations, departmental meetings, conferences with your subject supervisor, and the like are examples.

3. *Your school.* Sometimes secondary teachers are so steeped in their own major subject that they consider other subjects in the school of little importance. Avoid that attitude. On the other hand, don't think that the other subjects are more important than the one you teach. Science, foreign languages, English, mathematics, and so on—each area has its significance. For practical purposes add an essential ingredient to your ability to teach—the determination to master your subject.

4. *Yourself.*   You need a solid foundation of scholastic preparation. During a good lesson there are sidelights and references that constantly come up. The unexpected turns in a classroom discussion frequently reveal your mastery of your subject. Keep up on your subject and educational trends by subscribing to appropriate periodicals, by purchasing and reading professional books, and by active participation in professional meetings.

### 5. *Your attitude on going to your supervisor for help.*

Supervisors generally are aware that beginning teachers often need help, and supervisors frequently go out of their way to make suggestions. However, because of the pressure in secondary schools the amount of time that a supervisor can devote to an individual teacher is usually limited.

*As a general rule try to solve your own problems.*

To help yourself, take notes of important matters at departmental and faculty conferences. Keep these notes in your file for future reference. When you meet situations with your own resources, you tend to develop your abilities. For the average problem use your head, and you can usually handle the situation.

There are occasions, however, when you need assistance. If so, follow this order of priority:

1. Your "buddy" or cooperating teacher (an experienced teacher who helps a beginner).

2. Your subject supervisor (chairman, head of department).

3. The student's guidance counselor (grade adviser).

4. The supervisor of discipline (dean, assistant principal).

Also, of course, confer with the school psychologist, social worker, or attendance officer whenever necessary. In general take advantage of expert counseling. In the matter of control —sometimes the major problem of teachers beginning in a difficult school—don't go to the supervisor of discipline if you can solve the situation yourself. *Such an attitude builds confidence in yourself to maintain class control, the cornerstone of successful teaching.*

## 6. *Your attitude toward your community.*

Frequently beginning teachers get their start in towns where the influence of the community is felt more directly than in the cities. In many cases definite standards of conduct for teachers have been established. As a rule it is not advisable to offend the community's mores in regard to public drinking, dating racy characters, running up unpaid bills, remaining aloof from community organizations, fleeing town every weekend, and generally making it obvious that you do not wish to conform to what is expected in the way of conduct. Remember that if later you decide to change to another school system, it is helpful to have an excellent recommendation.

# CHAPTER 11

# Attitudes To Help
# Your Students

### 1. Your attitude on looking up a student's record.

As mentioned previously there are times when you may have to look up the citizenship and scholarship record of a student. Your approach should be to get a *complete* picture rather than finding evidence which will justify your complaint against him. For example, consider his background in addition to his marks and demerits. Check his attainments in such items as ability scores, reading grades, aptitude tests, and the like. When you tell him that you have checked his record, take the attitude that he can make himself worthwhile even when your investigation shows that he has failed in self-control and subject matter. **NEVER SLAM THE DOOR ON AN ADOLESCENT.** Remember, he is an immature person. This is not to say that you permit inferior work or poor behavior. It emphasizes, rather, what your attitude should be.

### 2. Your attitude on penalizing students. Five requirements. A warning. Four pressures to help you. Five general rules. Three important suggestions.

An infraction of behavior or failure to prepare homework may necessitate that you penalize offenders. The effectiveness of your teaching usually depends upon firm but pleasant management. Teen-agers for the most part have little respect for a teacher who can't control them. Nor do they admire a grouch. As a general rule you should be certain of these requirements:

1. That the penalty can be enforced. Don't put yourself out on a limb by insisting on a penalty that is ridiculous. Although previously mentioned in another situation, this advice needs to be emphasized under this topic.

2. That *you* are going to collect the penalty *yourself*. Thus, a student reports to *you* after school. He hands *you* his make-up work. A small point, but important to the adolescent. It convinces him that you are personally interested in his making good.

3. That you rarely threaten punishment. Usually give a penalty immediately or don't give it at all. Threatening adolescents is frequently worse than an empty gesture. It tends to weaken your authority.

4. That you are not handing out a penalty because you are in a bad mood. It is understood that there may be times when you lose your temper and feel like wiping the floor with a defiant teen-ager. Watch this. We all snap and growl on a rough day. Teen-agers don't mind just punishment, but the "mood bit" doesn't ride well.

5. That you have a standard set of penalties which applies equally to one and all. Your students will customarily esteem you for this. Thus, no homework means making it up after school. A little sass entails a telephone conversation with one of the parents that evening. Of course downright impertinence may call for a conference with the school disciplinarian. Strive to make the punishment such that the student will learn thereby that what he has done is not to be tolerated—and that it should not be tolerated. He should learn the limits of permissibility.

Coming to your assistance are four pressures. You may find it helpful to use them. They are:

1. *Parents.*   Generally speaking parents are interested in their children's progress through school. Usually you find them cooperative. As a rule don't wait for the day or evening set aside for parents to visit the school. It may be advisable to keep in constant contact with them where there is a problem student.

2. *Group.* Strive to master the technique of having the class develop an *esprit de corps* by constantly referring to it as a unit. Use this pressure to make the misbehaving youngster fall into line. It is frequently very effective with an adolescent.

3. *Promotion.* You may find the reward of promotion especially forceful at the end of the term. Graduation in the final year is usually also a boost. With the barn in sight, the horse goes faster. This is not to imply that you use a student's unacceptable behavior as a weapon to jeopardize his marks. As previously stated, grades should not be based on behavior. However, promotion or graduation in themselves are usually powerful rewarding stimulants to the average student.

4. *You.* Try to develop your rapport with the student difficult to handle. Customarily make it a personal challenge to your ability. If you are sincere and try hard enough, you have a good chance of helping him learn self-control.

Five simple rules to guide you are: First, be alert, especially at the beginning of the period. Second, correction should be immediate. Third, no favorites. Fourth, make penalties as easy to enforce as possible. Fifth, make penalties frequent but slight, rather than few and harsh.

The previous simple rules may give you better control and help prevent disastrous situations from developing. Such prevention is especially important in difficult urban areas where classes may be large or may tend toward misconduct. Let us discuss a few of the suggestions at greater length:

1. A few minutes detention after school means more than the threat of failure at the end of the term in nine cases out of ten. Furthermore, the younger the student, the more this is likely to be true. It is largely a matter of being inconvenient for the youngster. It generally means that he has to do without the company of his pals on the way home. A few minutes does the trick. Detaining him for an hour or more is pointless. Then you have reached the stage of punishing yourself. You may find it good strategy to mark papers and enter grades when he reports. This procedure is generally an effective yet simple means of enforcing control.

2. It is your obligation to see that the assignment is not too lengthy or difficult because then it may not be done. In addition, be careful to make the correction for failure to do the work fit the need. For example, the penalty for not reading assigned material may very well be to make a written summary of the missed assignment as well as the current ones until you feel the habit of doing assignments promptly has been formed.

3. A reprimand is surprisingly effective in many cases. It is advisable, however, to give the reprimand—especially if a severe one—*after the class has gone*. If other students stand around your desk, insist that they leave the room. Adolescents are sensitive to their fellows watching them being reprimanded. If rebuked publicly, they often become defensive or even abusive and this sometimes makes the situation worse. In addition, try to make your reprimand to the point. *Don't sugar-coat and don't exaggerate*. Adolescents are quick to perceive either. One advantage of this device is that repetition in most cases does not diminish its effectiveness. Instead, constantly bringing the misbehaving youngster up short at the end of the lesson usually brings results. Such reprimands become annoying to him, and so he ceases to be annoying to you.

And a final word: Keep your ears open for penalties used by other teachers. *Consider them carefully before making them part of your procedure.* The unruly teen-ager sometimes found in the average class and frequently found in the difficult class should be managed skillfully. Of course he is seldom found in superior classes.

### 3. *Take the attitude that a student does not understand. Four suggestions.*

A common error is to think that a student understands material in your lesson when he really doesn't. Indeed, sometimes he doesn't know that he doesn't understand. It is usually when you begin to prod with questions that the weakness becomes evident. Along the same line, you are likely to assume that a student has background for your subject which he does not in fact possess, for example, reading and comprehension skills. The assumption of knowledge makes a difficult situation for a student because an important characteristic of an adolescent is his reluctance to face up to a lack of knowledge for fear of appearing stupid before his classmates. He nods and smiles and goes through the gestures of accepting whatever it is that he is supposed to accept. "Are there any questions?" you ask. No hands are raised, so you assume everything is clear. *As a matter of fact, it rarely is.* Usually only superior students, whose accomplishments are not in doubt, have the courage to ask for an additional explanation.

Try the following suggestions. You may find them very helpful:

1. Ask probing questions throughout the class as checkpoints.

2. When you locate a student who doesn't understand, *call on his classmates to make the material clear to him.* This procedure pins down other students who may not understand thoroughly. *Your explanation should be held in reserve as a last resort.* Make certain the student now understands by having him make a summary. Emphasize that this procedure is a matter of class cooperation. One for all, all for one. It usually has a strong appeal to teen-agers.

3. Give credit to students who ask leading questions that will help the slower students to understand.

4. Make an analysis of the situation. Did the student not comprehend because of an inability? Or was it a matter of not doing his homework? If the problem is poor preparation, that is a different matter—one that calls for a conference with the youngster.

These four suggestions—like others throughout this book —apply not only to the formal lesson, but also to other techniques. *It is essential that every student understand what he is learning.* Take nothing for granted. This rule applies to *all* types of classes including shop, laboratory, art, and music.

*4. Your attitude should develop a respect for the dignity of each student. The personal touch. A caution.*

You should realize that an adolescent usually has become aware of himself as a young adult. He wants the world to acknowledge his new-found dignity—exaggerated, ridiculous, but to the teenager struggling to express himself, a precious attribute. In general his response to you frequently becomes a matter of individual loyalty. He often takes the attitude that if you respect him, he will respect you. To forget this principle may be to invite difficulties with an adolescent that could be easily avoided.

*Gracious personal touches are appreciated.* For example, make it a rule to make a pleasant comment to each student as he enters your room. A smile. A nod of greeting. Tell the young lady you like her new hair-do. She probably spent an hour fashioning it, hoping that it will be noticed and impress everyone. Or the girl with a new necklace, or pretty earrings. Tell the young man that his taste in jackets is excellent, or that you notice he's smiling more than he used to and he looks handsomer. *These are legitimate approaches that will inject into your teaching a warm, genuine, and personal element.*

Strive to make your relationship not teacher versus student, but teacher plus student. This attitude is not a compromise on strong control but a strengthening of it. Thus, avoid sarcasm, a factor that commonly alienates the student and usually gains nothing. If in exasperation you happen to slip and say something nasty, as soon as you realize your blunder, apologize. You will gain stature in the eyes of your students.

*Caution:* Use the friendly approach *without familiarity.* There is a distinction and you should walk the line carefully. Friendliness is usually invaluable but familiarity is almost always detrimental. Generally speaking to pose as a buddy is an invitation to disaster. To be an inspiration is a compliment. All of us have tucked away in our memory a teacher, here and there to be sure, who inspired us.

### 5. *Develop a pleasant attitude. Honestly, can you be sure you're not a grouch?*

For the most part students detect your attitude toward them with incredible accuracy. Admittedly there are teachers who do not measure up to the ideals of our profession. They are not sincerely interested in their students. Their object is frequently merely to earn a living. Uninspired, they often become embittered. Don't permit their bitterness to poison your attitude. Teaching is an outstanding profession. It requires no apologies.

Put yourself in the group of those who dedicate their lives toward doing a good job for the youth of America. Perhaps this sounds banal, but actually it is the real meaning of being a teacher. You cannot expect to inspire your students unless you project yourself as their leader in a worthwhile venture. An adolescent is attracted by a firm but warmhearted attitude. He is at a sensitive, imaginative level. Formulating his values, he reaches toward the sympathetic *leader,* not the namby-pamby who does not know the meaning of the word devotion. *Here is one of the most important factors in controlling teen-agers.* There are times, of course, when the situation demands that you be stern, but basically have a genial smile, a pleasant attitude, and positive loyalty to your students.

### 6. *Your attitude should reflect that you are a well-mannered person.*

You have a position in the lives of your students that demands that you conduct yourself properly. In particular avoid vulgar speech, coarse mannerisms, or indiscreet actions. Remember that a single carelessness can leave an unfortunate impression. You are constantly implying to them what they should and shouldn't do, therefore they will notice any infraction that you make. In particular be on your guard at social functions and sport events held by the school. You are expected to be relaxed but your conduct should be exemplary. A stiff-necked admonition but one that is sometimes necessary.

*Section Four*

# YOUR SUPERVISORS

*As a rule your supervisors are interested in making you an effective teacher. In most instances they know that good teachers often, but not necessarily always, achieve excellent results in respect to marks. Grades usually depend a great deal upon the ability of a class. On the other hand they realize that teachers who master the technique for enabling students to pass examinations sometimes fail to achieve other objectives of education that may be more important—the lasting effects that frequently make a person remember some teachers as guiding forces in his life.*

# CHAPTER 12
# *Working with Your Supervisors*

## *1. There is a school to run!*

In the teaching profession, as in any other, there are sometimes persons with conflicting personalities who frequently need to be blended by supervisors into a smoothly functioning staff. For example, a teacher with a swollen sense of his own importance may have to change his viewpoint.

Thus don't consider your personal needs to be more important than those of the school. Although you may have considerable latitude in the presentation of material and insertion of your personality into the dynamics of your lesson, you should strive to follow departmental and faculty regulations.

Fundamentally, a supervisor needs to consider his entire organization, not just a particular teacher. *For the most part align yourself with the aims of your supervisor.* This is not to say that every supervisor is able and all-knowing. But as a *beginning* teacher it is advisable that you generally accept his leadership. It may help to remember that most secondary schools strive —within their means—to provide the best education possible for adolescents, and usually supervisors keep that well in mind.

*2. What should you expect from your supervisors?*
*An evaluation of your position.*

By the nature of his position a supervisor commonly looks upon the school from a viewpoint different from yours. It may be advisable to keep this in mind when you hear your fellow teachers expressing themselves about their supervisors. Remember that as a rule criticism is easy to give and constructive suggestions are difficult to obtain.

Generally speaking each supervisor's obligation differs according to his position. Frequently he is a specialist with a definite goal in mind. For example, the guidance counselor tries to see that each student pursues a program best suited to his individual abilities. The subject supervisor ordinarily checks that each of his teachers is following the syllabus and giving proper instruction. The college adviser strives to place a graduate as best he can with the student's record. The supervisor of discipline endeavors to make sure that every student behaves himself. The attendance officer watches for truancy. All of these are specialized services designed to give more efficient help to students and teachers so that various phases of administration will be met. Obviously this is not a simple procedure. For its effectiveness your cooperation is customarily needed. As noted repeatedly, teenagers should be managed with a sure hand, and your supervisors from the principal down are working toward that goal. For efficiency a division is ordinarily made: subject matter for departmental meetings, school procedure for faculty conferences. The basic approach of the supervisor is usually to furnish specialized assistance to either the student or you, as the need may be. Your position, on the other hand, is generally to satisfy the demands of your supervisors and meet the needs of your classes.

3. *The importance of working with your super-*
*visors to solve problems. Six examples.*

You may find a constant complainer in your school. Often his
wails are long and loud. He frequently strives to indoctrinate
you against your supervisors. There are, of course, sometimes
justified complaints and possible needs for improvements. However, these should be taken up with your Teachers' Interest Committee, your Union Representative, or directly with the proper
supervisor, if there is no union organization. (Some schools are
antiunion.) But *don't be a self-appointed grievance watchdog who*
*growls at every opportunity.* Your supervisors are basically struggling to solve school problems. Most supervisors are usually
sincerely working for a smoothly running organization. In fairness reserve in your mind an area of reasonable latitude. Supervisors, being human, frequently make errors. Mistakes may occur,
but don't exaggerate them. As a general rule a secondary school
presents a complex situation. Commonly your problems are with
students, whereas the supervisors have to consider teachers, students, and demands of the community. In most instances you
make your job easier by cooperating with your supervisors, for
example:

1. *Passing in halls.* Help maintain order as students
go through the halls to enter their next classroom. In a matter
of three or four minutes, situations can develop that may lead
to a disturbance if not actual danger.

2. *Lavatory problems.* Take the trouble to supervise
lavatories briefly but effectively. If off duty, check as you go by
that a lavatory is not a meeting place for the Teen-Age Club to
have a smoke, swap stories, and discuss their affairs. In some
schools assignments are made for teachers to supervise lavatories.
A man stepping into the boys' room can clear it in a minute.

A woman going into the girls' room can accomplish the same result. The realization that a teacher may appear at any moment discourages overstaying.

3. *Cutting classes.* If you have a free period and are walking down the hall, stop students whom you see and ask if they have passes. This helps eliminate cutting. Make it a rule to challenge a student who seems to be loitering.

4. *Assemblies.* When you take your class or your homeroom (register or section room) to an assembly program, conduct them in order and with promptness to their proper place in the auditorium. Students are likely to get out of line and carry on considerably, or "cut-out" as the saying is.

5. *School projects.* Support drives to promote athletics and club activities, school shows, school magazines, school newspapers, and school dances. These extracurricular activities represent an aspect of school life that is stimulating to the student. Help make these undertakings not only financially successful but rewarding to the students by developing school spirit. Finally, frequently *participate in after-school life. Give of yourself.* The students truly appreciate it.

6. *Miscellaneous.* Whenever a situation presents itself as obviously needing teacher control, step into the breach. Help run the school properly.

*4. Adjusting to your supervisor. Do you make life difficult?*

Of course each supervisor has a different personality, so study him. Try to follow his way of thinking. Generally speaking, experience is on his side as well as authority. For the most part take positive action not only on what he wants done but in the way he wants it done. Demonstrate that you are working in a cooperative spirit. If you are given an assignment, make it a habit to do it *gracefully* and *with dispatch*. You might as well, if you have to do it anyhow. Otherwise, you possibly face an unfavorable rating. It is generally not advisable to develop a tongue-in-cheek response to directives. Such a spirit is often detected. On the other hand, for practical reasons don't hide your talents under a basket. Express your ideas to your supervisor so that he knows your interests and abilities. Even if your suggestions are not accepted, you have demonstrated that you are interested in what is going on in the school.

Of extreme importance is your attitude after you have been corrected by a supervisor for some failure on your part. *Don't carry a grudge!* In general a supervisor knows that you are going to make mistakes. Usually his correction has that in mind. Frequently what he is doing is to help you improve yourself. In most instances take the correction as another step in your professional advancement. We all have to learn—mostly by the way of hard knocks.

*5. Clerical work required by your supervisors. Three groupings. Ten suggestions to handle this bugaboo.*

Reports and records are a necessary part of your duties and *they should be both prompt and accurate.* Three general groupings are:

1. *In the homeroom.* A recording of attendance, lateness, truancy; mailing of absence post cards, report card writing, filing of excuse notes, and the like.

2. *In the classroom.* Attendance checked against the absentee list for possible cutting; marks entered for recitations, laboratory or book reports, examinations, and such. Many schools require that marking books be kept for eventual filing.

3. *In general.* Special items for the office. For example, many principals require that you evaluate all your students for personality traits on a permanent rating sheet.

These duties may total to a considerable amount of clerical work. Here are some suggestions that may help you to efficiently discharge this burden:

1. When taking attendance in your homeroom (register or section room), first enter absentees lightly in pencil. When the register period is over, make final entries in ink. This precaution often avoids crossing out entries made in ink, presenting a neater record.

2. If you make an error in your official attendance book, *do not erase.* It is generally preferable to cross out an error in ink and write the correction above it in ink so that *both error and correction are clearly shown.* Also, write your initials together with date of entry. This is a legal matter. Attendance records are important because of compulsory attendance laws and state-aid formulas.

3. Mail post cards to parents of absentees. (This may be handled by the office.)

4. Truancy reports. If in doubt, send one. (This may be handled by the office.)

5. Count the students present. The number absent added to those present should check with your register.

6. A capable pupil secretary is frequently of great service. In some schools students receive credit for assisting a teacher. However, a pupil secretary may *never* handle any *official record,* such as attendance, *unless authorized by the principal.*

7. Double check your count of attendance with your pupil secretary. It may be embarrassing when a student claims he was present and you've marked him absent, or vice versa, particularly when he can support his claim by evidence from his classes. You should be *sure.*

8. Start making out report cards as soon as possible so that they will be done accurately and distributed promptly. When they are returned, *check the parent's signature.* Also, verify that grades were not altered.

9. There may be forms that should be sent. For example, a letter to the parent of a student who failed two or more subjects, a request for the parent to interview the guidance counselor and you, or an invitation for parents' day, and so on.

10. Do it now! Make it a rule to *complete your reports as you go.* Remind yourself that clerical work should be done promptly. Make notations on your desk calendar. Seldom go out of school until *all* reports are handed in. *Make this an almost rigid rule.* It is especially applicable for items such as attendance reports, truancy slips, entry of marking-period grades, and report cards.

# CHAPTER 13

# Avoiding Unpleasant Situations with Your Supervisors

*1. What do the principal and subject supervisor expect? Four pointers on each.*

The principal wants you to cooperate with him in maintaining the standards set for the school. His problem is to see that the organization of his school is functioning properly. His mind is oriented to the fact that there are many rooms in the building and in each room there is a class with its teacher. He holds conferences with the various subject supervisors to make certain that all classes are running smoothly. Indeed, he may frequently visit classes himself. If a weak spot is located, it is his obligation to see that it is eliminated as quickly as possible. Bear in mind that some secondary schools have thousands of students and may present an extremely complex picture of administration. The principal is generally responsible for seeing that everything is in order. As a consequence, he usually expects cooperation every bit of the way. In general he cannot tolerate a teacher who is unwilling to do his share in carrying the load. Some pointers that may be helpful to keep in mind are:

    1. Be willing to acknowledge authority.

    2. Carry out instructions as given. The principal does not want your embellishments and modifications.

    3. Be on time at your assigned duties. The principal

must see that students have a teacher in charge at all times.

4. Don't require supervision. If you have a lunchroom duty, don't be sitting in a corner reading a newspaper. If you are assigned to proctor an examination, don't bury yourself in the latest best seller.

The subject supervisor's viewpoint is centered on instruction in his own department. His authority is primarily in your classroom. It is generally his responsibility to see that subject matter is taught properly and that satisfactory results are obtained on examinations. He is, to put it another way, particularly concerned with your effectiveness as a *teacher*. He therefore will probably check on some or all of the following:

1. Are your lessons fully prepared?
2. Are your students mastering your subject?
3. Will you cover your syllabus on schedule?
4. Are your results at the end of the term satisfactory in percentage of students passing in each class?

### 2. Do you look upon your supervisor as friend or foe?

The fundamental duty of the superintendent, principal, and subject supervisor is to run the school efficiently, not to persecute you nor to cultivate your friendship. Naturally supervisors desire a pleasant relationship with the faculty. However, their position is executive, acting as agents for the Board of Education to supervise the instruction of adolescents. Usually the principal rates his new teachers twice a year until they achieve tenure.

You may hear cries of persecution or favoritism from some teachers. Such possibilities can exist. But isn't that too frequently the way of the world? Whatever justification there may be, play your cards close to your chest. *When you have a problem, discuss it with the proper supervisor on a practical basis.* For some reason there are some teachers who seem to expect a charming afternoon-tea atmosphere when these matters of school business come up. This is generally the wrong approach. Consider the end result. Both the supervisor and you have the same goal, the welfare of the students in your classes. In most instances, come directly to the point.

### 3. Beware of personal or departmental feuds. The way out.

Unfortunately, sometimes you may be trapped in quarrels between teachers or departments. It would be pleasant to say that such serious disagreements don't exist, but they occasionally do. Generally speaking, individual feuds are caused by a person unable to work harmoniously with his fellows. Everything has to go his way or he is not playing. On the other hand, departmental quarrels result from various causes such as overlapping of syllabus material in related areas, teachers carrying split programs that put them into two departments during the same term, clash of personalities between subject supervisors, and so forth. It is understandable that you like to feel closely affiliated with your department, but don't get embroiled. An important key to your effectiveness as a teacher is your relationship to your fellow workers. Remember, a feud usually brings frustration and unhappiness that can be frequently avoided by discretion.

### 4. When your supervisor comes to observe your teaching. Some suggestions to ease your tensions. The need for a conference.

It it natural to be nervous when the principal or subject supervisor visits your room and spends either a full period or only a few minutes. Of course when he observes your teaching for a whole period there may be an additional strain. At a time such as this, your lesson plan is usually your best friend. Thus we reemphasize, plan your work and work your plan. You may find a repetition of the suggestions previously given helpful if itemized again. Use the following as a check list for easing possible tensions:

## 1. ROOM CONDITIONS

a. Are the windows adjusted for proper ventilation according to the weather?
b. Are the lights on?
c. Is the floor clean? Even a few pieces of scrap paper give your room an untidy appearance.
d. Are the boards erased at the end of the period?

## 2. TIME FACTOR

a. Start your lesson promptly.
b. Keep track of the time. Frequently check your watch against the progress of your lesson. Thus at the end of twenty minutes, you should be about half way through.

## 3. MOTIVATION

a. Make a definite effort at the start of your lesson to show the reason for teaching it.

## 4. CLASS PARTICIPATION

a. Remember to skip around, giving everyone the opportunity to contribute to the discussion.
b. First call on a weaker student, then on a brighter student for comment.
c. Do not call on more than three successive students if it is obvious that the class doesn't understand the point you are trying to make. Reorganize your presentation by putting the question in a different way or using another approach.

## 5. BOARD USE

a. Whenever possible have students illustrate or summarize the issues of the lesson by using the boards.
b. Don't hesitate to use the board yourself if an item is not clear.

## 6. SUMMARY

a. The major topics should be recapitulated in an evaluation. Usually it is also advisable to have a midsummary.

After the lesson is over, the supervisor may customarily arrange for a post-teaching conference, but if he does not, it is usually advisable to make an appointment with him to get his reaction to your lesson. At the conference make notes of favorable as well as unfavorable comments. In many cases a written report is given, but personal observations give better insight. Try to contact your supervisor the same day if possible, while the impressions are fresh in his mind, for a more clear-cut picture. However, some supervisors feel that the conference is better deferred for a day or so until you have had an opportunity to calm down and do some self-evaluation. Remind yourself that the sooner you remedy errors in your teaching technique, the better. In order to bolster your ego, remember that none of us is perfect. In the case of many beginning teachers, *the most valuable assistance you can get is an honest appraisal from your supervisor.*

### 5. *Why you shouldn't complain about your classes. Six advantages in having a difficult program!*

In most instances don't cry on your supervisor's shoulder. He usually knew what your classes were like before he assigned them. Program exigencies often leave him no choice. But having difficult classes has some advantages:

1. Your subject supervisor as a rule appreciates what you are doing. You generally will find him cooperative in discussing problem cases.

2. The situation is a challenge. You frequently learn how to manage many difficult class issues.

3. Obviously if you can handle troublemakers, you should find it easy to control normal classes.

4. The subject supervisor customarily will make an allowance for you in your final averages. He understands the predicament you are in. His primary concern is in your ability to do effective teaching in the larger sense of achieving the broad objectives of education.

5. A good job done with an uphill fight usually earns the admiration of both the principal and subject supervisor. Understandably you will probably rate as a strong teacher.

6. The teacher who demonstrates his ability to cope with *all* types of instructional situations is generally the one who eventually may be favorably considered when there are openings in the lower supervisory echelons, such as deans, guidance counselors, and coordinators.

*Section Five*

# YOUR FELLOW
# TEACHERS

*You occupy no lonely bench in the profession of teaching. You are part of a team that is fighting for a good education for all students. You cannot remain on the side lines even if you so desire. Other teachers' goals necessarily become integrated with yours. Department and faculty conferences are expressly designed to consolidate what is best for your particular school. Thus in most instances cooperation is a meaningful word in your relationship to fellow teachers.*

# CHAPTER 14

## Pointers for Professional Well-being

*1. The visiting teacher idea. Six check points. Four ways to profit from your observations.*

In an earlier chapter we suggested that you study teaching techniques of fellow teachers. Get their permission to observe them when you have a free period. It may prove helpful if you check the following points in particular:

1. What new ideas are presented?

2. Was there a constant challenge to the class?

3. Would you consider presenting the material in this manner to your own classes?

4. Make a notation of techniques used that you liked. Which of these do you wish to adopt for your own use?

5. Where did you think the lesson was weak? How would you correct the shortcomings?

6. Would you rate the lesson as excellent, satisfactory, or poor? Why? Be specific.

If at all possible, arrange for a meeting with the teacher giving the demonstration so that you can be sure you understand the structure and grasp the high points of the lesson. Here are four generally recognized ways to profit from observations:

1. Write up the lesson you observed. Imagine that you are a supervisor and making a detailed report.

2. Come to definite conclusions. Locate the weak and strong points.

3. If you visit another school in the same city, or if you teach in a small town and visit a school in another town, make reports to your principal and subject supervisor on the results of your visit. They want to know how the observation helped you. Of course be sure to thank the teacher(s) you visited —express appreciation for the privilege.

4. Put new ideas to work *immediately*. Weave them into your lesson plans.

### 2. *Department meetings. Six ways that they help you.*

Many matters come up that concern only your department. For example, for unification of efforts decisions have to be made on books and other materials, on content of examinations, on syllabus revisions, and such. Some of the ways that department meetings may help you are:

1. You are aware of what is going on in the department for procedures and materials.

2. You have a sense of working with others to achieve common goals such as training slow learners, challenging the talented, and developing club programs.

3. You commonly know what topics to cover in a particular assignment.

4. You frequently have a schedule indicating how much content you should cover by a certain time.

5. You can usually get help in teaching techniques for your subject if you need someone to turn to. Almost always some teachers in your department have had some experience in your particular problem.

6. You often know when certain audio-visual material is available for your use. A schedule for such material is usually decided. Thus there is generally no doubt as to who gets what and when.

### 3. Take notes of important items at faculty conferences.

Sometimes the principal has mimeographed sheets distributed as a guide for discussion during the conference. If so, make notes on the margins of significant points. If you have to refer to these instructions, your notations will help make the matter clear. Of course if no guide sheets are furnished, take your own memorandums. Conference notes should be filed according to date. From time to time you may have to refer to them to be sure that you are getting everything done as it should be.

### 4. Teachers' organizations have four functions in your professional life.

You may find it helpful to note that there is a quadruple benefit when you belong to organizations dedicated to teachers' interests:

1. Goals that consider the welfare of your students, such as provisions for the physically and mentally handicapped, remedial reading, speech therapy, guidance, and the like.

2. Aims centered on benefiting *all* teachers. For example, better school conditions, pension benefits, improved salaries, legal representation, and so forth.

3. Some associations specialize in specific help in a particular subject area such as for teachers of English, science, or many other subjects.

4. Teacher organizations usually give you a sense of unity from belonging to a large enterprise in which many thousands of persons are directly concerned and offer their best talents. You become more aware of what is professionally vital— a live wire and not a dead connection.

One of the hazards of teaching is that you may become an isolated person who thinks only of himself, his immediate day's instruction, his forthcoming pay check, and has no large horizons for professional development. Participate in activities so that you have a share in formulating goals and achieving them.

### 5. Search for stimulating contacts. Some suggestions.

Strive to keep hungry for fresh ideas for creative teaching. Seek new approaches for presenting your subject in an interesting manner. In our profession there is rarely such a thing as standing still. If you do not thrust yourself forward, you usually slide into a rut. It is advisable to provide yourself with stimulating professional contacts. You may find that *good* education courses are frequently invigorating and often very helpful. These generally fall into four groups:

1. *Content courses.*   Make it a rule to strengthen your competence in your chosen specialty. Almost always, advanced content courses enrich your professional life.

2. *Educational psychology and sociology.*   Contact the latest thinking on understanding the human element with which you are dealing all day throughout the school year.

3. *Methods.*   Look for new ways of presenting old material. This is a search that should never end.

4. *Supervision.*   If you are ambitious to further yourself and become a supervisor in the teaching profession, get an early start in this area.

In addition you may find it worthwhile to have the following in mind: First, start working toward an advanced degree. Generally speaking, the higher your education, the more salary you can command. Second, provide for cultural advancement. This side of your development should be nourished. For example, travel. Third, enter into community enterprises. They present a genuine stimulus. They give you the opportunity to cultivate worthwhile persons in your community.

Your goal: Maintain yourself on a high level of professional advancement to become a well-rounded, progressive teacher.

### 6. Is the grass greener in the other teacher's lawn?

When you see a fellow teacher smiling in the halls, when you listen to him laughingly discuss his classes, when you talk to his students, you may come to the conclusion that he has all the breaks. Indeed, it may be true. But it could be that he is a better teacher. And so we make excuses for ourselves. Ninety percent of the time the difficulty is not so much with the classes as with the ability of the teacher.

Perhaps you think you have the worst building assignment. For example, your lunchroom duty is more arduous than another teacher's study hall. Of course duties vary in difficulty, but the supervisor of assignments usually rotates them so that they are evenly distributed.

Or you believe your subject supervisor is more demanding than those in other departments. (Remember, it is the province of the principal to bring supervisors into line when justified.) A general observation, however, is that the more control a subject supervisor injects into his department, the more efficiently it probably will run, and usually the less difficulty you will have. Strong supervision as a rule makes your job easier.

### 7. Your professional library. Five values. Seven ways to build it.

It is sometimes said that none of us is self-sufficient. If you rely solely upon your own ingenuity you very possibly limit your development. Thus you may find that the reading of professional books and magazines is of inestimable value, for example:

1. *Lesson plans.* Get ideas for different presentation and find interesting supplementary material. Magazines in your subject area are especially helpful.

2. *Reference.* Frequently you need to check on data.

3. *Background.* Look for an additional means for giving a firm foundation to your teaching. Brings an overall development.

4. *Personal expansion.* Unless you appoint yourself as a committee of one to see that you mature in professional growth, you very possibly may stunt yourself.

5. *Timeliness.* Keep up to date for the newest thoughts in educational matters.

All of us have different amounts of money available for purchasing books and magazines. The best guide is to consider professional material as *essential.* A carpenter or mechanic needs a complete set of tools and so do you. As a minimum, set aside fifteen dollars a year. This amount is small in comparison to your total income, and it usually won't be missed. On the other hand, it gives you a foundation for building a professional library. Unfortunately, some beginning teachers fail to make even this modest provision.

Some suggestions that may prove helpful in ways to start are:

1. Obtain book catalogues from publishers specializing on education in general and your subject in particular. This is a prime source frequently overlooked by new teachers.

2. Other teachers, especially those in your department, will frequently make suggestions.

3. Your subject supervisor often has considerable knowledge in this area. Practically every day he gets circulars, advertising leaflets, approved lists, and the like.

4. At faculty conferences the principal sometimes suggests books or articles. Investigate these.

5. Contact your school librarian. Almost always she is an excellent source for suggestions on the latest worthwhile educational books. And of course go to the public library.

6. Professional magazines in your particular subject. For example, if you are a history teacher, a periodical dedicated to social studies.

7. Newspapers, especially the Sunday supplements, sometimes carry critical reviews of the latest books in your field as well as in the general area of education.

# CHAPTER 15
# *Meeting Personality Problems with Other Teachers*

*1. We're all different. Five points to keep in mind. Gossiping buddies. Another problem.*

It is not the purpose of this book to attempt an analysis of the various types of persons. You are aware that people are different and that sometimes they present personality problems. Generally speaking you may find it helpful to note these five suggestions:

1. *Expect differences in personalities.* Ordinarily no two teachers handle contacts with personnel in the same manner.

2. *Notice obvious problems.* Let's be honest. Some personalities rub us the wrong way.

3. *Should get along.* Even though some individuals on your school staff are incompatible with your personality, you have to march with them—at least to the extent that you are able to do your job properly.

4. *Tolerate other viewpoints.* From our contrasting personalities and environments we frequently build very different attitudes. It is rather unreasonable to expect all the other teachers to dovetail into our concepts.

5. *Value clashing personalities.* Frequently a contrary temperament presents a stimulating challenge.

In some schools it seems that there are gossiping buddies who slap you on the back and carry tales. They are customarily a nuisance. Perhaps the best treatment is to quickly change the subject. A good general principle is not to talk about fellow teachers unless what you have to say is in the nature of praise.

Another problem sometimes is the teacher who appears deliberately antagonistic. Such an attitude is expressed in a number of ways, but you get the message. In most instances study him carefully. It is possible that you may have offended him in something you least expect. Usually it is advisable to speak to him directly about it. *Your success in your profession depends a good deal upon your ability to get along with your fellow teachers.* It does not mean that you have to be subservient—merely that a challenge exists and you should meet it.

## 2. *Stepping on toes. Some advice.*

A teacher interested in science would customarily defend the importance of chemistry, earth science, physics, and biology. An English teacher speaks for the values of poetry and composition. A language teacher appreciates the need for modern languages in our complex world. If you downgrade the importance of the other teacher's subject, you can scarcely expect him to have a sympathetic attitude toward you.

In the same manner, don't offend teachers in your department. Sometimes a chemistry teacher feels that his subject is of more importance than biology, or the earth science teacher may believe that his subject is better for the average student than physics. Even in a particular subject there are often different methods of presenting the same material. As a general rule don't get into a heated argument over how to teach *Romeo and Juliet.*

Then, too, there is frequently an opposing opinion on the relative value of topics within a syllabus. For example, in earth science one teacher may believe that the astronomy unit should be minimized and weather expanded, and another teacher would reverse the emphasis. A discussion is stimulating, a quarrel is sometimes destructive. Whatever the disagreement, your attitude should allow for individual differences of opinion.

In summary, if possible avoid stepping on professional toes whether between subject areas or within your own department.

### 3. Does jealousy gleam in your eyes? Three ways to promote fellowship.

Although you are paid a salary, you ordinarily like to feel that your services are appreciated. Sometimes it may seem that you do not receive sufficient praise. You possibly observe that other teachers get excellent commendations. You wonder why you do not receive the same acknowledgment for what you have done. But inequalities of recognition are almost certain to occur. However, if you have a cooperative attitude toward doing things for the students and for the school, it is usually only a matter of time until your supervisors become aware of your contributions. Meanwhile try to avoid green-eyed pangs. In the main, work for fellowship with other teachers. Three areas you may find especially worthwhile to promote are:

1. Take part in enterprises such as faculty shows, student-faculty games, and the like.

2. Assist other teachers in putting on assembly programs.

3. Cooperate in special exhibits that require participation by a number of teachers such as art displays, musical recitals, and such.

*4. The substandard teacher. Three cautions.*

Almost all of us strive to achieve the best results we can. But there is sometimes the individual who apparently has no intention of doing any more work than he is forced to do in order to get his pay check. Ordinarily he is easily detected. Here are a few cautions that may prove good advice:

1. Don't let a shirker influence you. He is often a subtle yet frequently devastating contact.

2. Affirm that you believe in fulfilling your professional obligations. It may be helpful to let him know your creed.

3. It is customarily not your place to wrangle with the substandard teacher. For practical purposes let the supervisors handle him.

*5. What do your fellow teachers expect from you? Four suggestions.*

Your fellow teachers commonly have a right to expect high performance and an excellent standard of behavior from you. Essentially it frequently boils down to a matter of shared responsibility. The following suggestions are some of the ways:

1. *Esprit de corps.* Present a solid front with the faculty to the student body.

2. *A shared room.* Leave your room in suitable condition for other teachers to use. Furthermore, don't monopolize the equipment, supplies, closets, and desk space.

3. *Committee work.* At the beginning and end of the term everyone should cooperate so that all work is finished on schedule. Examples of committee work are programs for stu-

dents, transcripts for colleges, office records, extra help for guidance counselors, and so forth.

4. *Toleration.* Occasionally you may have a complaint from a teacher. Ordinarily don't go running to the boss carrying a tale of woe. Of course there are occasions when matters develop that should be brought to the attention of a supervisor. As a general rule anything detrimental to students or which seriously interferes with your efficiency as a teacher should be dealt with authoritatively. But usually a few amiable words can set matters right. And then, too, there are minor differences that you can often afford to overlook entirely.

*Section Six*

# YOUR CHECKUP

*It is possible for you to be something of a failure
as a teacher even though you have perfect control in
all your classes and every student passes his final
examinations with flying colors. Consider the
subtle yet positive effect of your character and
personality on the development of your
students. Tomorrow your teen-agers take their places
in life as young men and women. See through your
own problems to evaluate yourself as an effective
teacher in those terms. If your students on graduation
day were making out a report card on you, how
would you rate in terms of inspirational leadership?
Did you contribute something beyond learning
self-control and scholarship? What factors of character
building did you supply to help them in their
preparation for adulthood?*

# CHAPTER 16

# *Checking on Your Own Problems*

*Note:* In the final chapters we again run into a stream of suggestions that have largely been presented before. But once more they are in a new context, and it may prove helpful to consider them from a different viewpoint. Teaching situations interweave many ideas, attitudes, and applications so that isolation of single factors without repetition is frequently not advisable if a beginning teacher is to have a helpful understanding of the whole situation.

### 1. Are you discouraged? Two factors to keep in mind.

When you mark your students' examination papers, you may be shocked at the number of low grades. You were so sure that the results would prove that you had done a good job. In such a moment, especially if a high percentage fail, it is usually wise to revamp the questions or else rate papers first by *scores* and then convert these into equivalent *marks*, thus, 75 = 90. Consider the following:

1. Some guidelines to help you check on your effectiveness are the following.

a. The kind of students you have.
b. The difficulty of your examinations.
c. The success of your students in other classes.

2. The nature of teaching seldom permits obtaining complete evidence of your success. *You rarely know exactly how much progress you made.* The important ingredient is hardly ever cold passing percentages. Rather, the warm, vibrant adolescents maturing into manhood or womanhood are largely the measure of your success.

3. Many rewards of teaching should be looked at in perspective—an accumulation that builds over many years. Gradually your teachings become a part of many hundreds of homes.

## 2. *Are you qualified to be your own critic? Three guiding questions. Your daily report.*

Don't make the mistake of resenting criticism, of having your feelings hurt, of believing that the supervisor should have a sympathetic attitude toward you. A principal or subject supervisor is entitled to opinions as to what he wants to see in your lesson. His viewpoints are ordinarily supported by years of teaching experience. It is usually up to you to satisfy his demands as best you can.

When you give your lessons each day, imagine that he is sitting in back of the room making an observation. Also, periodically review previous observation reports. *More than anything beware of self-satisfaction.* Form the habit of evaluating your lessons by checking yourself on these points mentioned repeatedly because of their importance:

1. What are you demanding from the students?
2. What are the students looking for from you?
3. Did **BOTH** do their share?

It may be helpful if you write the above questions on a slip of paper and clip them on your seating plan. *Check them constantly, until they become a part of every lesson.* Thus you have a continuous critical analysis of your teaching. Indeed, sometimes it is worthwhile to make a *written report to yourself.* It may help to put your finger on your good and bad points. Generally speaking this daily appraisal serves to give assurance that you are teaching better every day.

### 3. Do you know the teacher's golden rule? Two crucial attitudes.

Tremendous power is vested in you as a teacher. Students pass or fail according to your judgment. Sometimes college admission depends upon your recommendation. Therefore, it is generally considered unfair to use grades as a club to maintain control. The golden rule is: *Maintain positive control and at the same time give generous marks.*

Keep in mind that nothing succeeds like success. This principle is particularly true in dealing with adolescents. Although the following advice has been mentioned, it is so vital to your success that at this point it may bear repetition:

1. Demand firm control whether a student passes or fails.

2. Make every effort for each student to get the top mark his ability can reach.

If you fail a high percentage of students, there is usually something wrong. Most likely either the material is beyond many of the students put into your class, or you are a poor instructor. The situation is unfortunate when a student is faced with a subject that is too difficult or when he has an incompetent teacher. Strive to see that every student who enters your room is interested in doing the work, is able to handle the subject, and does the very best he can. *Follow through.* It may help to bring the results you want.

## 4. Can you keep the you in yourself?

Every school day you are in contact with hundreds of teen-agers and dozens of fellow teachers. We have discussed methods for getting along with them, but it is also important that you preserve your own personality. *Each of us usually has one or more contributions to make.*

Strive to work harmoniously with student body and staff, but recognize that you are entitled to be an individual. A weak personality has little to offer students, faculty, or supervisors. Keep the you in yourself alive.

## 5. Should you leave school work in school?

Teaching usually demands a tremendous amount of emotional energy. For a fresh start each day, many experienced teachers follow this rule: *Finish everything that has to do with school in school.* If necessary, go early and stay late. Even at midterm or final examination time, mark papers in school. Their view is that if you go home burdened with hours of paper work every night—five days a week, month after month, year after year— you'll be worn to a frazzle and come to look upon your profession with loathing. Of course there are exceptions when some work must be done at home. On the other hand, many superior teachers prefer to take work home with them and do it at their leisure. If you choose to take work home, be careful not to carry it to the extreme so as to interfere with your at-school competence. The point is, keep yourself a vital person with wide interests whose life is a sparkling adventure. If you do, you will be a much better teacher.

6. *Are you under constant nervous tension? Six approaches.*

Avoid leaving school every day exhausted from emotional strain. But it is no simple matter to have effective control over some 150 adolescents in your classes, plus more teen-agers in your assignment period, plus the pressure of your own inexperience and the need to meet the requirements of your supervisors. All this puts a burden on your nervous system. To help eliminate tension consider the following:

1. Write a list of situations that make you nervous. Note that these are so obvious that you are conscious of them. Take them one at a time. Come to a decision on how to eliminate or minimize each stress.

2. Subconscious strains are frequently difficult to identify. They vary according to personality. What annoys you may be a triviality to another teacher. Study yourself. Search for your weak spots.

3. At the end of each class ask: Are you nervously upset? What caused it? Once you locate the pressure, try to do something about it.

4. Adjust your mind to the fact that there are likely to be some tensions during the day. There are almost certain to be incidents, but assure yourself with a serene attitude.

5. The need to get work accomplished by a definite date sometimes puts stress on you. Use your calendar to plan ahead.

6. Major nerve strain often comes from lack of class control, inability to get along with certain faculty members, or a conflict with a supervisor. Refer to the many specific suggestions in this book. Some of them may prove helpful.

# CHAPTER 17

# *Evaluating Yourself as a Teacher*

## *1. Do you have a sense of dedication?*

Dedication is not a matter of coming to school at dawn and staying until sunset, although that may sometimes be necessary. Rather, dedication is an expression of your sincere interest in the welfare of your students. Thus, the suggestions made in this book are but a means toward establishing guidelines to help you work with teen-agers so they may achieve scholarship and character. Consider putting one of the following on the first page of your plan book:

1. A poem or quotation that inspires you.

2. A reminder that in your classes are tomorrow's men and women, and that the service you perform reaches far and wide.

3. A statement of your professional creed. A challenge to the best in you.

You may be one of those who feel that a written expression of dedication is ridiculous—it is what is in your heart that matters. Be that as it may, a sense of devotion to your students must be within you to become a genuine teacher.

## 2. *What are your responsibilities?*

What you owe the community varies a great deal according to the locality in which you work. Social and economic factors in a small town are customarily unlike those in a large city. Your responsibility toward parents will usually be evidenced in the parent-teachers association and in individual contacts.

But more important is your responsibility to your students. A sense of protecting their interests, of being a part of their lives. Years later when you meet them in the street, you realize the significance of your responsibility. Your major reward is not in salary, nor is it in commendations from the principal for excellence in teaching, but in the person who comes to you, whom you meet in the store after ten years, who says, "Remember me?" and there's a big grin on his face. And you look at this man and wonder who he is and when you taught him. But he remembers you and feels that you have an affinity with him and his life. You do. Make no mistake about it. Even more so when his children come to your classes.

Your major responsibility: To understand that you have a responsibility.

## 3. *Have you a correct appraisal of your position with the students?*

It is easy to get the idea that you are indispensable to your classes. On the other hand you may feel that your teaching is of little value. Actually your path is usually between the two. You have tremendous significance, but you have limitations. It is often in the placing of yourself in true relationship to your students that you may have your greatest difficulty.

You play a meaningful part in the lives of many teen-agers for a large part of their day. What you say and what you do is generally important to them. At the same time, realize that adolescents have outside interests. Strive to get a balanced viewpoint.

### 4. *Do you enjoy teaching?*

If you believe that the students in your classes are so much garbage, if you think of them as a bunch of bums, and if you believe that your efforts are a waste of time, then you are finished. You may stand in front of a class, spout facts and collect answers, but you are not the person who should be there. When you hear a teacher always complaining about his students, the fault is usually with his analysis. This is not to say that whatever teen-agers do is to be condoned. Of course not. But many of them come to you with severe handicaps from environment and heredity. Neither factor is their fault. Strive to develop the attitude that you want to help these youngsters as much as possible with the handicaps they have. *Look upon them as if they were your sons and daughters.* Somehow this perspective makes you enjoy teaching.

### 5. *What is your idea of a successful teacher? Your two viewpoints.*

Some teachers measure their success by the scores their students get on examinations. Others think that social adjustment is the factor to consider. Common sense dictates that either viewpoint forced to its conclusion is ridiculous: a brilliant scholar lacking in group adjustment or a social butterfly who fails all subjects.

Your concept of a successful teacher should be to get all students to work for intellectual goals to the best of their abilities, and at the same time to make sure that they are well-adjusted. To evaluate yourself use two viewpoints:

1. Success in each day's teaching. Did you accomplish what you set out to do that day?

2. Success at the end of the school year. Were the scholastic and social results satisfactory?

## 6. How important are you in your school?

You teach a particular subject to a definite number of adolescents. Unfortunately, some teachers get the idea, for one reason or another, that their subjects, problems, and students are the beginning and end of the school. Absurd, but their demands upon other teachers and upon the supervisors reflect that attitude. The opposite viewpoint, not being alert to your importance, may also be detrimental. When you are absent, your place must be filled immediately because your work cannot be eliminated.

Generally speaking neither exaggerate nor minimize your value. Don't expect special considerations because you are you. On the other hand, don't be afraid to ask for materials for your classes. Evaluating your position is a middle-of-the-road process. You are needed, but you can be replaced. Study your faculty. You probably will reach the conclusion that some teachers are overbearing and others shy. True, one should allow for personality differences. This appraisal gives you in your own terms a picture of your importance. Although only one cog in the school's wheel, you are essential.

## 7. Do you have an expanding horizon?

Sometimes teachers feel that they have "arrived" and that there is no need to worry about their personal development. They wrap themselves in a cocoon of do-nothing-more. But teaching is a dynamic profession. It requires the warmth of an expanding horizon so that the years bring increasing vision. Make certain that you are not becoming small-minded, groveling over trivialities, distorting the charming aspects of your personality. Don't bury your worthwhile characteristics in the sand of hum-drum routine of from-class-to-class existence.

Your personality needs nourishment or it shrivels to a husk of nothing to offer the adolescent. Oddly enough, it is your strongest weapon in providing leadership for your classes. Teen-agers are quick to note the teacher who has a broad outlook on life. *Set up a program for personal development.* Start immediately. Procrastination means that you may possibly retire into a shell of smug self-complacency.

Don't permit your spirit to shrink into a has-been. *Remember that you are increasingly farther apart in age from your students as time goes by.* Therefore, it becomes progressively more important to keep spiritual contact with the adolescents you are teaching.

# CHAPTER 18

## In Conclusion

### 1. Perfect answers for all possibilities?

You deal with a large number of adolescents. Every day each of them is changing. In addition conditions within your school are in constant flux. Thus pat solutions for all problems are beyond you. To expect cure-all procedures is foolish. Because students are personality composites and situations usually complicated, perfect answers become rarely possible. As mentioned in the preface, there are limitations. But *reach for a fundamental understanding of your students* and *the ability to handle a difficult situation.* No one expects you to be perfect, but *everyone expects you to be sincere.*

If you asked a dozen architects, all of superior ability, to make drawings for a model home, each would almost certainly produce contrasting plans. Similarly, a dozen lawyers would probably present different briefs for a trial, or a dozen doctors may disagree on the treatment for an illness. So, too, teachers have their own ideas on a school problem. *Seldom is there one best method.* Only experience will enable you to evaluate your personality against difficulties. You may disagree with some of the suggestions made in this book. That is as it should be. But the major aim will be achieved: to offer suggestions which may help you.

## 2. *The challenge of your profession.*

Life is becoming more complex and along with it the organization in secondary schools is growing both in size and efficiency. Each department is specializing in ever-widening programs. New audio-visual aids, laboratory equipment, and teaching machines are thrusting themselves forward. Publishers are pouring out a steady stream of improved textbooks and material for better presentation of your subject and broadened educational understandings. Thus the challenge of modern secondary education requires alert teaching.

In addition your students may find it difficult to enter college as the competition becomes increasingly competitive. And in the business world good positions in the trade or commercial fields require more and more definite training. Because of these demands your students need all the preparation you can give them.

## 3. *Looking forward.*

As the years bring you ever-increasing experience, hold tightly to the spirit of youthful enthusiasm. Don't become so engrossed with increased competence in your teaching that you forget to enjoy a laugh with each class every day. Sharing laughter is so important. And don't become the sage talking down to your youngsters— talk *with* them. Because then you will keep the sense of what youth thinks and feels—the heart of secondary school teaching. For you need to give and take with each new tide of teen-agers if you hope to keep their interests sparkling in the sunshine of a warm teacher-pupil relationship. Successful rapport with adolescents carries the price tag of sincere good will. In the years ahead, keep your affection for your youngsters always burning brightly. Give them not only inspiration but also the memory of a full measure of devotion.

# SUGGESTED READINGS

This handbook is intended as a guide for immediate assistance when you begin your career. It must, by its nature, be limited in scope. It would defeat its purpose if it went into considerable detail. Therefore, charge yourself with a program for reading books that specialize in the various aspects of your professional growth. A few suggestions which cover a broad area follow. For an extended list, write to publishers of professional books on education. Some are suggested with their addresses.

## METHODS

Alcorn, Kinder, Schunert, *Better Teaching in Secondary Schools*, Holt, Rinehart and Winston, 1964. 9.50

Bossing, *Teaching in Secondary Schools*, 3rd ed., Houghton Mifflin Company, 1952. 7.75

Brown, *Student Teaching in a Secondary School*, 2nd ed., Harper & Row, 1969. (Although written for the student-teacher, it contains many excellent ideas.) 5.50

Grambs, Iverson, Patterson, *Modern Methods in Secondary Education*, Holt, Rinehart and Winston, 1958. 9.50

Hoover, *Learning and Teaching in the Secondary School*, 2nd ed., Allyn and Bacon, 1969. 7.95

Klausmeier, *Teaching in the Secondary Schools*, 3rd ed., Harper & Row, 1967. 9.95

Muss, *First-Aid for Classroom Discipline*, Holt, Rinehart and Winston, 1964 (pamphlet). 1.95

Rivlin, *Teaching Adolescents in Secondary Schools*, 2nd ed., Appleton-Century-Crofts, 1965. 6.00

Stiles, McCleary, Turnbaugh, *Secondary Education in the United States*, Harcourt, Brace & World, 1962. 7.95

Wiggins, *Successful High School Teaching*, Houghton Mifflin Company, 1958. 6.75

## PSYCHOLOGY

Anderson, Ausubel, *Readings in the Psychology of Cognition*, Holt, Rinehart and Winston, 1965. 8.95

Baller, *Readings in the Psychology of Human Growth and Development*, Holt, Rinehart and Winston, 1962 (paper). 6.95

Cronback, *Educational Psychology*, 2nd ed., Harcourt, Brace & World, 1965. 8.95

DeCecco, *Human Learning in the School*, Holt, Rinehart and Winston, 1963 (paper). 6.95

Havighurst, Taba, *Adolescent Character and Personality*, John Wiley & Sons, 1965 (paper). 1.95

Klausmeier, *Learning and Human Abilities*, 2nd ed., Harper & Row, 1966. 8.95

Mouly, *Psychology for Effective Teaching*, 2nd ed., Holt, Rinehart and Winston, 1960. 8.95

Redl, Wattenberg, *Mental Hygiene in Teaching*, Harcourt, Brace & World, 1965. 7.95

Staats, *Human Learning*, Holt, Rinehart and Winston, 1964. 9.95

Stephens, *Psychology of Classroom Learning*, Holt, Rinehart and Winston, 1965. 9.50

Trow, *Psychology in Teaching and Learning*, Houghton Mifflin Company, 1960. 7.95

## GUIDANCE

Glanz, *Foundations and Principles of Guidance*, Allyn and Bacon, 1964. 7.95

Miller, *Foundations of Guidance*, Harper & Row, 1961. 6.95

Mosher, *Guidance—An Examination*, Harcourt, Brace & World, 1965. 3.25

Ohlsen, *Guidance Services in the Modern School*, Harcourt, Brace & World, 1965. 8.25

Sachs, *The Student, the Interview, and the Curriculum,* Houghton Mifflin Company, 1966. 5.95

### SUBJECT TECHNIQUE

*English*—Morsey, *Improving English Instruction,* Allyn and Bacon, 1965. 8.50

*Language*—Meras, *A Language Teacher's Guide,* 2nd ed., Harper & Row, 1962. 6.25

*Physical Education*—Cowell, Schwehn, *Modern Principles and Methods in Secondary School Physical Education,* Allyn and Bacon, 1964. 8.50

*Science*—Thurber, Collette, *Teaching Science in Today's Secondary Schools,* Allyn and Bacon, 1964. 11.35

Washton, *Science Teaching in the Secondary School,* Harper & Row, 1961. 7.75

*Social Studies*—Hunt, Metcalf, *Teaching High School Social Studies,* 2nd ed., Harper & Row, 1968. 10.25

### MEASUREMENT

Ahmann, Glock, *Evaluating Pupil Growth,* 3rd ed., Allyn and Bacon, 1967. 8.95

Green, *Teacher-Made Tests,* Harper & Row, 1963 (paper). 2.25

### GENERAL

Combs, *The Professional Education of Teachers,* Allyn and Bacon, 1965 (paper). 2.95

Gallagher, *Teaching the Gifted Child,* Allyn and Bacon, 1964. 7.95

Havighurst, Hunt, Morris, Wrenn, et al., *Becoming an Educator,* Houghton Mifflin Company, 1963. 7.50

Kirk, *Educating Exceptional Children,* Houghton Mifflin Company, 1962. 7.50

Kirk, Johnson, *Educating the Retarded Child,* Houghton Mifflin Company, 1951. 6.75

Kneller, *The Art and Science of Creativity,* Holt, Rinehart and Winston, 1965 (paper). 2.50

Otto, McMenemy, *Corrective and Remedial Teaching,* Houghton Mifflin Company, 1966. 6.75

Stinnett, Huggett, *Professional Problems of Teachers,* 2nd ed., The Macmillan Company, 1963. 7.25

Wittich, Schuller, *Audiovisual Materials,* 4th ed., Harper & Row, 1967. 10.95

Woodring, *Introduction to American Education,* Harcourt, Brace & World, 1965 (paper). 1.95

## PUBLISHERS

For your convenience, addresses of publishers of suggested books are given below. For additional publishers of professional education books, consult your librarian.

Allyn and Bacon
     470 Atlantic Avenue
     Boston, Massachusetts 02110
Appleton-Century-Crofts
     440 Park Avenue South
     New York, New York 10016
Harcourt, Brace & World, Inc.
     757 Third Avenue
     New York, New York 10017
Harper & Row, Publishers
     49 East 33 Street
     New York, New York 10016
Holt, Rinehart and Winston, Inc.
     383 Madison Avenue
     New York, New York 10017
Houghton Mifflin Company
     2 Park Street
     Boston, Massachusetts 02107
The Macmillan Company
     866 Third Avenue
     New York, New York 10022
John Wiley & Sons, Inc.
     605 Third Avenue
     New York, New York 10016

# Index